HISTORIC HAUNTS
of the
SOUTH II

JAMIE ROUSH PEARCE

THE FOURTH BOOK IN THE
HISTORIC HAUNTS SERIES

Inquiries should be addressed to:
Jamie Roush Pearce
historichaunts@yahoo.com

BOOKS IN HISTORIC HAUNTS SERIES:
Historic Haunts Florida
Historic Haunts Florida II
Historic Haunts *of the* South
Historic Haunts *of the* South II

Foreward:

In this book I tried to include any and all personal experiences I had at each of the locations I've written about. Unfortunately, ghosts, as I like to say, do not perform on que. In situations where my personal experiences were limited, I tried to interview people who lived or worked at the locations, past or present. Hours of research, traveling to the different locations, visiting, investigating, touring, and interviewing, all went into writing this book and I loved every moment of it! I have heard a lot of fascinating stories, experienced a lot of paranormal activity, and have made new friends. The trouble with putting this book together was not how to find and investigate places in the South, but how many I could squeeze into one book! I covered a lot, but also left a lot out, I soon realized I would need to write another. So be on the lookout for part III, where I hope to make it up to those states and places I may have excluded.

Dedication:

First I want to thank my amazing hubby Deric for all his help and encouragement. I couldn't do it without you sweetheart.
Xoxo
Jamie

I also want to thank all the locations and everyone who has helped with my Historic Haunts series. Without the owners and staffs at the locations it wouldn't be possible. I also can't forget the ghosts, without them, there would be no Historic Haunts.

Special Thanks:

Assistant Investigator: Gayel Roush

Editing: Deric Pearce & Paula Dillon

Design and Layout: Deric Pearce
All images unless otherwise credited are provided courtesy of the author
Additional photography provided by and copyright Big Stock

First Printing December 2014

HISTORIC HAUNTS OF THE SOUTH II

Table of Contents

THE GHOSTS OF OLD BRYCE

Old Bryce Mental Institution, Tuscaloosa, Alabama

Construction began on Old Bryce Mental Institution in 1853 and opened for patients in 1861. It is the oldest and largest inpatient psychiatric hospital in Alabama. It was modeled on reformist psychiatric ideals that have only recently become standards.

It was named after Peter Bryce, a South Carolina psychiatric pioneer, who demanded patients be treated with respect and kindness no matter what their illness was. He discouraged and ultimately abandoned the use of strait jackets or restraints altogether in 1882. Instead he advocated treatment through programs and activities like farming, sewing, maintenance, and crafts. He set a standard for treatment of the mentally ill that was recognized around the country, and followed for years.

The legacy of Bryce wouldn't last. By the twentieth century the patient population expanded drastically. Standards of care for the patients and the monies to do so were not top priority to the current government's agencies and facility employees. New workers at the hospital paid very little and lacking resources didn't have the compassion for the patients that the earlier care takers had shown.

By 1970 the hospital had more than 5,200 patients residing in the facility never meant to hold that number. Alabama at that time, ranked last among US states for funding mental health. Deplorable conditions led members of the media to compare the hospital to a concentration camp. This was especially true for disproportionately large numbers of African American patients who were often abused and treated worse than their white counterparts. Despite the terrible conditions at the facility it was added to the National Register of Historic Places in 1977.

A lawsuit brought about in 1970 on behalf of 15 year old Rickey Wyatt (a resident of Bryce) would set wheels in motion that would forever change the conditions and treatment of the mentally ill in the US. Through legal actions and court ordered agreements a set of federal minimum standards for the care of people with mental illness or retardations in institutional settings was created. Known as the "Wyatt Standards" they contain four basic criteria for care:

1. Humane psychological and physical environment
2. Qualified and sufficient staff for administration of treatment
3. Individualized treatment plans
4. Minimum restriction of patient freedom.

In December 2009, plans were made to relocate Bryce Hospital to a newly constructed building and have the, eager to expand, University of Alabama take over the campus. As of this writing the construction of the building is expected to be

5

completed in the fall of 2013. In the meantime, many of the patients have been sent to group homes and community care. Tough fiscal decisions about the care of the mentally ill loom ahead for the Yellow Hammer State, but are believed to be achievable in cooperation with the University of Alabama.

Old Bryce's Ghosts

Apparently some of Bryce's old residents decided to stay here even after passing. Students and faculty of the University despite not fully taking control of the campus as of this writing have already reported hearing the sounds of disembodied sobbing in some of the rooms. Others have reported hearing ghostly screams as if someone is being mistreated or tortured.

Other visitors to this former facility have reported strange odors floating through the air, phantom lights, hot and cold spots, furniture moving on its own, and phones ringing in rooms where there are no phones. Transparent forms in old hospital gowns have also been seen walking the halls in places that were common areas while the facility was still a hospital.

Even though the early days of the hospital were caring and compassionate, it seems the hospitals dark days are what have stained the atmosphere here. It has left such a heavy and sad imprint that may never go away. Let's hope that moving forward a bright future and some relief will come to Bryce's mentally ill, both living and dead!

THE GHOSTS OF THE GRAND OLD LADY
1886 Crescent Hotel, Eureka Springs Arkansas

Photo courtesy of the 1886 Crescent Hotel

Nestled in Eureka Springs Arkansas, is an amazingly and lovingly restored hotel known as the 1886 Crescent Hotel. The hotel has certainly seen a colorful bit of history and activity, and apparently still does. Besides being able to boast about visits from celebrities and presidents, and once having a cat as a hotel manager, the building has been called the Grand Old Lady of the Ozarks and "America's Most Haunted Hotel". That's certainly enough to catch the attention of this Historic Haunts fan.

History of the Crescent

From 1886 to 1901 The Crescent Hotel was operated by the Eureka Springs Improvement Company and was an exclusive hotel open year round and catering to the carriage set. The hotel featured a stable with one hundred horses for guests to ride. The hotel also featured afternoon tea and evening dances with parties practically every night enhanced of course by the in house orchestra.

In 1902 the Crescent was leased to the Frisco Railroad for a five year time period. By the end of the railroad's lease business had begun to decline. In 1908 with the hotel experiencing slow winter traffic, the decision was made to open Crescent College within the hotel grounds. For the next 26 years this college for woman and the hotel that housed it would serve the public. By 1934 the depression had impacted the Crescent and the college and the hotel were closed.

The hotel reopened in 1937 under the control of new owner Norman Baker. He turned the building into "Baker Cancer Hospital and Health Resort". Baker was a

7

millionaire inventor who called himself a doctor. Unfortunately, he lacked proper medical training. He lured patients with claims of having discovered several "cures" for many deadly diseases. Part of his alleged cures included drinking the fresh spring water and breathing the fresh air (not that uncommon as mineral springs and other such novelties were considered beneficial to many people). What most people and patients didn't know was that Baker had been kicked out of Iowa before moving to Arkansas for practicing medicine without a license. When he relocated to Arkansas he moved many of his cancer patients with him. In actuality Baker killed rather than cured many patients, and the former hotel basement became the morgue housing the dead and a horrific assortment of severed body parts.

In 1940, Baker went to jail for fraud for four years and his "hospital" was closed down. In 1946, John R. Constantine, Herbert Shutter, Herbert Byfield, and Dwight Nichols took over this wonderful building and tried to restore it to its once happy state. The building was renovated and converted to serve the community as a hotel once again. It continued to serve the community in this capacity until March 15th, 1967 when the 5th floor and most of the 4th were claimed by fire.

Dwight Nichols and the hotel were saved from certain disaster by a successful lawsuit in 1968. The Crescent was sold again in 1972 and again it went through restorations and renovations. It reopened May 1st, 1973 with a wonderfully restored interior and boasting Morris the cat as the hotel "manager". The hotel would enjoy many successful years highlighted by a Willie Nelson concert in 1982 to a past capacity crowd, and a Bill Clinton banquet speech in 1985. In 1992 a banking crisis forced the hotel into foreclosure. In 1994 Morris the cat passed after a 21 year stint as manager.

The Crescent was again purchased in 1997 by Marty and Elise Roenigk and they started a 6 year restoration and renovation project. Marty and Elise over saw the addition of a conservatory, wedding court with fountain garden, cottages, and jacuzzi suites. Marty passed away in 2009 but Elise still owns the hotel. With such an interesting past, it's no surprise that the Crescent has a few ghost stories to tell.

Haunted Ghosts of the Crescent

The first paranormal entity attached to the Crescent pre-dates the opening of the hotel. A good-looking Irish stone mason named Michael fell to his death during construction near what is now room #218 "the most popular room at the hotel". His ghost has been encountered and reported numerous times. Michael is apparently still a fan of the ladies and is often reported sharing his wanted or unwanted paranormal affections by touching, pinching, and the like.

Besides Michael there are three other spirits believed to be attached to the

Possible spirits at the 1886
Photo courtesy of the 1886 Crescent Hotel

hotel's early days. The first is a little girl that allegedly fell to her death from the 4th floor railing. She is often encountered in the hotel and seems to favor the places in the hotel near the public restrooms.

The little girl's spirit is not the only child entity encountered at the Crescent. The spirit of a little boy wearing "pop bottle" glasses and wearing "old timey knickers" has been described by several witnesses. He is often seen skipping through the kitchen and the kitchen staff often blames this supernatural child for the pots and pans mysteriously swaying and clanking.

Another spirit often encountered from the Crescent's early days is believed to be that of Dr. John Freemont Ellis, a physician during the early era of the hotel. He has often been seen wearing a long black cut away coat, a cravat, and a top hat. He is described in such great detail that people often marvel at his mutton chop side burns. His pants are always described as grey striped, but fade out around his knees. He is often seen in the gift shop and seems to always disappear when noticed. His presence is sometimes marked by the smell of cherry pipe tobacco, something unusual for this non smoking property.

Hospital Era Haunts

During the Crescent's days as a hospital, stories from the time claim at least one patient committed suicide. This patient's apparition is often seen on the balcony looking very sad and depressed. Maybe she knew there was no cure and could not stand to suffer any long.

This isn't the only apparition and paranormal activity believed to be attached to former patients. Theodora, a former cancer patient of Dr. Baker's has been encountered and reported frequently looking for her keys. In addition, a mystery patient in a white wispy night gown appears in luxury suites and occasionally at the foot of the bed of hotel guests.

Patients aren't the only haunts at the Crescent. There are also many reports of ghostly dogs, (St. Bernards to be exact) which have been seen and felt at the hotel. Several guests have reported something rather large and furry resembling

9

K-9s rubbing up against their leg. Some witnesses have seen the dogs and others have only felt them. Many believed these entities are the ghosts of Dr. Baker's dogs. He was known to have several St. Bernards as pets.

The last apparition worth mentioning that is frequently reported at the Crescent is Baker himself. He has been described so well in most of these encounters that there is little doubt that it is him. He has been seen throughout the hotel. However, he is commonly encountered in the morgue area. To this day the former morgue frequently exhibits unusually high EMF readings with no obvious source and there are persistent reports and photos of strange mists and orbs.

Captured paranormal on film?
Photo courtesy of the
1886 Crescent Hotel

Finally, as if all this activity wasn't enough to solidify this Eureka Springs landmark as the country's most haunted, there are numerous reports in other areas of the hotel. These reports by workers, staff, and guests detail disappearing pools of blood, and glasses and bottles which rise from the spots on the shelves and crash to the floor (especially in the kitchen).

Whether you experience the paranormal while you are there, the 1886 Crescent Hotel is still worth a visit. This beautiful old building has been well cared for and it shows. It is a great piece of Arkansas' history and an intriguing Historic Haunt.

THE COURTHOUSE STANDS ACCUSED ...OF BEING HAUNTED

Old Clay County Courthouse, Green Cove Springs Florida

The Old Clay County Courthouse

Green Cove Springs is a small city unknown to many outside of the state of Florida. Those who do know of it may recognize it as the County Seat of Clay County or to some businessmen, the birthplace of Charles Merill of Merrill, Lynch & Company fame. However, the town has other fascinating points of interest, among these is the Old Clay County Courthouse. I first became familiar with the Courthouse through docent Vishi Garig and my team's investigation of the jail across the courtyard (see Historic Haunts of the South). While the jail continues to be a haunted hot spot for paranormal investigation groups (the jail, courthouse, and grounds were recently featured on a nationally televised paranormal investigation show); the courthouse is also a source of frequent reports of paranormal activity. So of course I wanted to look into more with my investigation team.

A History of Legal Preceedings

The original Clay County Courthouse was built in 1890 and was used for over 80 years. All the county business took place here in Green Cover Springs. Citizens got married there, paid their county taxes there, and trials were held there. Many criminals were sentenced here and some were convicted and faced the death penalty.

The courtroom has many windows along the front and several look out across the front lawn providing a view of the jail and the gallows. All the trials with the potential death penalty took place here and were carried out practically on the front lawn. In fact, at least five hangings and a suicide were thought to have occurred on the front lawn.

11

Today the recently renovated courthouse is used for teen court. If paranormal reports are to be believed though, it also seems to be housing a few ghosts as well. In fact, the entire area is available for rent for paranormal investigations. Because of the frequent activity it is a great place to train new investigators and get them accustomed to events that commonly occur during an investigation.

Evidence of Hauntings

Many investigators and groups have captured "Class A" EVPs (electronic voice phenomenon) here. We call these "Class A" because there is no doubt about what is being said by the disembodied voice. One of the spirits known to haunt the courthouse has been referred to as a "wise ass". Many paranormal groups have investigated this location and captured EVPs that seem sarcastic or insulting. C.A.P.E. is one of these groups. During one of C.A.P.E.'s investigations an EVP was captured calling one of the larger members of the team "fat". At least one of the spirits here at the courthouse is an intelligent one because he responds to specific questions or situations taking place in the building.

In addition to EVPs at the courthouse, there are frequent reports of of disembodied voices and conversations, and inexplicable shuffling noises. Further, people have reported seeing moving shadows in areas with no light source or person to explain them and full body apparitions in the hallway. In fact, many people at night standing outside of the courthouse have reported seeing shadows moving inside through the windows on the second floor in the courtroom even when the building is known to be deserted.

We had been told that several paranormal teams had much more activity when during investigations, they reenacted a trial. A mock trial seems to stir up more recordable activity. So this was definitely on our minds as we approached our own investigation.

Historic Haunts Investigates

When Historic Haunts Investigations had the opportunity in October 2013 to investigate the old courthouse we planned to try out the trial recommendation (among other things) and to our pleasant surprise we had a few experiences of our own. We arrived at the courthouse and began doing the scientific work common to many paranormal investigations like doing base readings of the building. In this case we were a bit more focused on the second floor. Base readings of EMFs (electromagnetic fields) and temperatures, let us know what is normal for an area and makes it easier to discover any abnormal readings. We also check for causitive elements that might debunk or help explain "paranormal" findings, these are elements like drafty windows and heating/air vents. These are all typical during investigations so that we will know our surroundings and more easily detect unusual elements or occurrence.

After our initial investigation and surveying we set up our full spectrum cameras in the courtroom and began doing a mock trial. We started getting unusual flash light activity on both random lights and control flash lights during our trial and then heard voices in the hallway. Unfortunately, as in many of the paranormal reports we were unable to make out what was being said. I first went into the room where I thought the voices came from (just outside of the courtroom) and the flash light on the judge's desk suddenly came on. When I went further into the room I was told the flash light was turning on and off quickly in the courtroom. A name suddenly came to me, Mr. Borden!

Gail Borden (1801-1874) was the founder of Borden Milk in 1853 and the former owner of the land before the courthouse and jail were built. I don't know how to explain it, but often times names, visions, or words will come to me during an investigation. I went back into the courtroom and asked, "Are you Mr. Borden?" The flash light suddenly turned on. I asked the contact or entity in the room to turn the light off so I could ask further questions and it did. I then asked, "Were you here before 1892?" The flashlight came on again and again turned off when I asked it to. I then asked, "Are you related to Lizzie Borden?" The light didn't turn on so I added, "If you are, it doesn't matter to me because I say she was innocent." As soon as I said this, the light started frantically going on and off!"

Further questioning yielded erratic and unpredictable responses in the flashlights, EMF meters, and EVP and other recording equipment. The mock trial did render interesting responses magnified when the "judge" or the "prosecutor" were acted out more forcefully. However, none of this abnormal and unusual activity was easy to trace to certain questions or causes. Eventually the responses ceased all together.

After the courtroom activity things got pretty quiet during the rest of the investigation. We covered the entire courthouse and it appeared the spirits were done for the evening with the exception of a few random EMF spikes. We searched and could find no explicable or obvious causes.

Overall, it was definitely an interesting investigation, especially since I have always had an interest in the Lizzie Borden case. We look forward to bringing the team back and perhaps enjoying a retrial. For fans of the paranormal this is one place in our judgement with a lot of appeal.

Court not in session

13

HARD ROCK AND HAUNTINGS
Hard Rock Café, Key West Florida

Key West is full of history, unique culture and ghost stories! As a matter of fact Key West is home to the only haunted Hard Rock Café in the world. The Key West Hard Rock Café is a beautifully restored three story Victorian home on Duval Street that was built by Florida's first millionaire William Curry (a reputable salvager) in the late 1800s. It was a grand wedding gift for his son Robert.

Hard Rock Key West

The Unfortunate Mr. Curry

Robert Curry was a bit of an unfortunate man. Despite being born into a life of wealth and privilege, he had a life of bad luck and a variety of maladies that kept him a sickly and somewhat depressed man. When Robert's father passed in 1896, Robert inherited the family fortune. Unfortunately, his newly acquired wealth did nothing to turn his luck or his health around.

Robert was known as a poor business man. Whether his business problems and his trouble managing money grew due to being sickly much of the time is a matter of debate. As Robert grew older, he became even more financially strapped and eventually the family inheritance was completely gone. This in turn caused his health to decline even more. In a fit of illness and depression he went to the second floor and killed himself in this home. There is much speculation as to the method of his demise. Some locals claim he shot himself, but most believe he hung himself.

A Hanging Surprise

During my first trip to Key West I played tourist not paranormal investigator, so I knew nothing about the story of Robert Curry. On this family trip I spied a Hard Rock Café situated in an old Victorian house and had to check it out. After having lunch there on the tropical patio and people watching on Duval Street with the family, I went inside to explore the former residence turned restaurant.

As a fan of the Hard Rock restaurants I was enjoying exploring the place and the many iconic pieces of memorabilia. When I got up to the second floor and towards the back of the building (away from the busy street) I noticed it suddenly became so quiet you could have heard a pin drop. The abrupt silence was extremely odd. I continued exploring into one of the back rooms when the atmosphere of the room began to feel very heavy and somewhat depressing. I felt my stomach turn over and that's when I saw a vision before me. I closed my eyes to make it go away and after a couple of seconds it did. What I saw was a man hanging from the ceiling by a noose.

I quickly went back downstairs and joined the rest of the family. As I sat down the waiter returned to the table and I asked him who was on the second floor in the back part of the house. He looked surprised and said, "You mean.....?" pointing to the place I had just been upstairs. I answered, "yes", and the waiter followed with, "He has been quiet lately. His name is Robert Curry a former owner. It is said he committed suicide in that back part of the house. Some say he hung himself others say he shot himself where the bathroom used to be up there."

Later that night we went on the Key West's Original Ghost Tour (hey I may have been on vacation, but I'm still a fan of the paranormal at heart) and wouldn't you know it, we stopped at the Hard Rock. The unfortunate story of Mr. Curry was relayed to us by our tour guide. My good friend and author David Sloan started the Key West tour in 1996, and is extremely well versed in Key West haunts having written several books on them. He wrote many of the tour scripts and so I had no reason to doubt our guide. David's knowledge of the Key West spirits and his extremely accomplished guides left me with no doubts that this was the best tour in the area. The guides confirmed that many of the tour guests have experienced paranormal things while at the Hard Rock Café.

Talking further with former tour guides and guests, I learned that many over the years have seen a man with dark hair on the second floor. The guides told me the man seemed to vanish into thin air right before their eyes. Most seem to believe its Robert Curry. A plausible idea since the description of the apparition seems to match photos of him. Besides the apparition, many people have also reported the feeling of dread or depression in the room where Curry took his own life. It seems that some of the darker and depressing emotions that may have caused Mr. Curry to take his life may have left an imprint on the room, or may be a signal to his spiritual presence.

My curiosity piqued, I had to do a little research myself. I discovered a multitude of paranormal incidents claimed to occur at the Hard Rock.

Cold spots have been felt throughout the restaurant especially the second floor and furniture has been known to move or rearrange itself. In addition, shadow figures have been reported and many visitors and employees have encountered frequent instances of disembodied whistling.

While you're in Key West check out the Hard Rock Cafe for yourself. You'll be treated to an absolutely amazing lunch or dinner and a possible ghostly encounter. While you're there soaking in the artifacts of rock's heroic and tragic figures, have a drink and toast to Mr. Curry.

WHAT IS MANIFESTING AT MEEHANS?

Meehan's Irish Pub, St. Augustine Florida

Meehans Irish Pub

St. Augustine is amazing! Well at least to me. Although, I admit I am somewhat biased having run a successful haunted tour business there for several years. The town is full of history and hauntings and I have several favorites. One of the spots that I definitely have a soft spot for is located right off the bay, Meehan's Irish Pub & Seafood House.

History of an Irish Pub

Long before the building now known as Meehan's was constructed, the lot was used for storage during the early Spanish Era of St. Augustine while the fort Castillo de San Marcos was being built. The current structure was built in 1917 and is thought to be at least the third on the site. The first home burned in the 1894 fire and the second in the 1914 fire. The current building was built by William Dismuits and his wife.

William was the first President of the First Florida National Bank. His wife was one of the reasons the coquina City Gates are still standing. She was a member of the Woman's Preservation Group who protested against the city tearing down the gates. The building would go on to serve patrons as a bar and restaurant. It would change names and hands several times finding popularity as Churchhill's Attic (among others) before later being bought and renovated by John Meehan. Today John still operates his namesake establishment and it is more popular than ever with the living and the non-living.

Tales of a Haunted Irish Pub

Before I ever investigated this iconic St. Augustine Pub I had a chance to hear about the paranormal activity first hand from owner John Meehan. When John bought the building it went through extensive renovations and according to him that is when unusual things began to happen at the restaurant and pub. During the renovations a picture of a woman from decades ago was found upside down and left that way off the wall. When John returned to the office he kept finding it hanging in the same position (upside down) on the wall. He would remove it before leaving and locking up and again find it hanging on the wall. All the while no workers at the site nor any other living soul claimed involvement, the mystery remained of who was doing it and why. This was particularly interesting since John had the only key to the office and made sure the picture was off the wall when he securely locked the door. John decided that someone or something obviously wanted the picture up on the wall. The picture now sits in a particular spot and no one is allowed to touch it. Since the picture's permanent relocation to the wall in an upright position, no further strange happenings connected to it have occurred. However, John's unusual encounters at the Pub go way beyond just the picture.

Another incident at Meehan's happened during renovations as well, when John came in and found the hinge pins not secured on a door. He didn't think too much of it, thinking that a worker had merely forgotten to secure them. John put the pins back in before locking up. The next day, the hinge pins were out again, and John once again put them back in. The following day the hinge pins were once again removed and this time the door was leaning against the wall. This phenomenon kept happening even when the workers were gone and John was the only one in the building. Eventually, John frustrated shouted, "Cut this sh** out!" It didn't happen again.

Other employees of the Pub have stories about it as well. Reggie Maggs another Meehan's staff member, also shared his account of seeing a woman in dark period dress walking through the lower bar with her hair pinned on top of her head. She didn't even seem to notice he was standing there; she just went about her business. She has been reported several times and seems to be a residual haunt since she routinely performs the same actions whether anyone is there or not, and doesn't interact with others (unlike whoever was messing with the door and hinge pins,which might be considered an intelligent haunt). The mysterious woman has been spotted in other areas as well.

One day, one of the staff was upstairs and saw the woman sitting by the

17

window at one of the tables looking out at the bay. The staff member went downstairs to get a server and when they came back upstairs the woman was gone. She appeared to be the same woman that Reggie had seen downstairs walking through the bar.

Historic Haunts Investigates

My first investigation here was February 16th, 2011 with team member Amy Mann, Meehan's staff member Reggie Maggs, and Dr. Harry Stafford Professor of Human Consciousness Studies. While sitting in the pool room, Amy and I saw something blocking the light coming from under the office door as if they were standing nearby it. We had been told the bar was empty and in fact Reggie was the only staff member present and was supposed to lockup when we finished the investigation. We got up to investigate and when we opened the office door, the room was empty.

Another unusual incident happened when we walked down the back stair case into the kitchen. It felt as though we walked through a vortex and into a furnace. We all got very dizzy and felt extremely hot, and this despite the fact that the kitchen had been shut down for hours and it was quiet chilly outside. The K2 EMF meter lit up into the red as we walked through what felt like the vortex before returning to normal. As we began discussing whether to leave the kitchen or not, we became very light headed and the room got cold with an icy breeze. It seemed as though something wanted us to leave the room.

We decided to leave the kitchen and go into the bar, shake the feeling off and recoup. Reggie went behind the bar to get us all a Coke for our now queasy stomaches, suddenly he turned wide-eyed and very pale. This caught our attention and we asked if he was alright. He looked up and informed us there was an usual shadow moving from left to right on the wall behind us that wasn't ours or his (especially since we were all standing still at the time). When we turned to look, it was gone.

We began to set up to do an EVP session upstairs at the table near the window where the female apparition had been seen. As we were setting up to do so I felt something brush against my leg. I didn't say anything because I thought maybe Amy or Reggie had bumped me under the table. Then Amy jumped and asked if I kicked her, then Reggie experiencing something similar asked as well. I hadn't kicked either of them. Then Reggie informed us that although less frequently reported, patrons and others had from time to time reported a ghost cat there roaming around the restaurant who liked to get attention by bumping into or rubbing up against people.

Throughout that evening and on subsequent investigations we have continued to have small unusual incidents and have picked up a variety of phenomenon with our equipment. So much so that we have been invited to return and investigate again. It is our hope that Historic Haunts Investigations will be investigating here again soon so keep an eye out on our website for details about our next investigation at this Historic Haunt.

A PENNY FOR YOUR HAUNTS

Penny Farthing Bed and Breakfast, St. Augustine, Florida

Penny Farthing Bed and Breakfast

St. Augustine, the nation's oldest and arguably the most haunted city is loaded with haunted bed and breakfasts. However, few can match the charming victorian atmosphere of the Penny Farthing Bed and Breakfast. This gem of St. Augustine's historic district dates back to 1897. The inn has weathered many changes and today is owned and maintained by a family from Yorkshire England as it once was in the 1930s. To say that the English know something of victorian charm is an understatement, but the current owners know something else, the place is haunted and very active.

Penny Farthing Tales

The Penny Farthing has had many reports of paranormal activity, unusual occurrences, and coincidences. One of the more interesting is that of a guest, who had heard nothing of the hotel or its resident spirits and yet described to a "T" a "psychic vision" she had of one of the house's entities. Even more interesting is that her description matched reports by other eye witnesses who had seen the apparition. The vision was of a little girl with long hair around the age of 4 or 5 years old wearing a sailor's style blouse with a big bow and a floppy hat. The woman had never been to the inn before and had no idea that this is the spirit that is often seen in the Cherry Room and is always looking for her mommy. Many people have been in this room and report hearing a little girl's voice say, "Mommy?"

The little girl's spirit is not the only entity reported at the house. Another apparition often encountered is a woman in a white dress stating that the house is hers! She

19

sounds very upset in her claim as if she doesn't know why strangers are in her home.

Historic Haunts Investigates the Penny Farthing

I was invited to bring my team down and investigate the inn in December of 2012. The owners reserved the attic room for our lodging and for our investigation. The attic room is known for having toy soldiers placed in the room appear and disappear often moving locations seemingly on their own. We went in to the room and dropped off our equipment noting the positions of the soldiers and left to have dinner before the investigation. When we returned to start unpacking our gear, eight toy soldiers were scattered in completely different locations around the room. We chalked this occurrence up to an interesting coincidence because someone could have set them up while we weren't there and the camera's weren't running.

Not thinking too much more about the soldiers we got our gear and started investigating the whole place. Unfortunately, like so many times, we were experiencing little to no activity. There are a variety of paranormal television shows on these days and sadly many have promoted a popular misconception to the public. Paranormal investigation is often made up of tedious hours of evidence gathering with a variety of equipment. In most cases, investigators capture little or no activity or evidence contrary to tv's quick edits that make it seem super active and exciting. Tonight, as is the case on many nights, we were getting no compelling evidence at the inn. I decided to call the investigation for the night and my investigators and I returned to our room. We all retired to our beds a bit disappointed making sure to set our cameras to record while we slept just in case.

In the middle of the night I awoke to the smell of lavender. I didn't think too much of it and the camera was still recording so I rolled over and went back to sleep. About an hour or so later I woke up to the sounds of an argument that seemed to come from the foot of the bed. I whispered over to Gayel, one of my team members, to see if she was awake and if she heard it too. She said yes. The discussion grew more heated and sounded like it was right in front of us. We saw nothing but could still hear the disembodied voices.

The next morning Gayel informed me that during the night while her legs were under the covers a cold breeze on her right leg had startled her awake. This was pretty interesting considering she had layers of blankets upon her legs and the sheets were tucked in leaving no means for wind gusts or circulated air to hit her leg.

As we started packing up the equipment we noticed the toy soldiers were in different places than they were when we went to bed. The next day we started reviewing the video that we thought had recorded the entire night. We would soon realize it had not. Even though the light was on the camera and it showed it was recording all night there was nothing on the film. Apparently the soldiers didn't want to be filmed and whoever was arguing didn't want it on camera either.

According to many paranormal accounts what my team and I experienced was nothing unusual. To many the Penny Farthing is known as much for its unusual and inexplicable paranormal activity as it is for its gourmet breakfasts and scenic porches. I hope to return to the Penny Farthing in the future and do a follow up investigation on this peculiar and compelling Historic Haunt

THE GORGEOUS GHOST OF MISS LILY
St. Francis Inn, St. Augustine, Florida

corner view St. Francis Inn

The St. Francis Inn is one of the St. Augustine's most historic landmark inns. In fact, its long history predates the founding of the United States. Reports of paranormal activity in this splendid inn have likewise continued for quite some time, drawing fans of the paranormal, ghost hunters, and history buffs. In November 2012, Historic Haunts Investigations investigated The St. Francis Inn for ourselves and had a few ghostly encounters of our own, but before we get into that perhaps a little background information.

The Historic St. Francis

The house was built in 1791 during the second Colonial Spanish Period by Gaspar Garcia. He was a military man and member of the 3rd Battalion of Infantry Regiment of Cuba. Garcia's house would have many owners over the years. In 1802, Juan Ruggiers a sea captain purchased the building, the home sold again in 1838. This time it was purchased by Colonel Thomas Henry Dummett of Barbados. He was an officer of the British Marines. One of Dummett's daughters, Elizabeth, married William Hardee an 1838 West Point graduate. Another daughter married Brigadier General Cochran. When Colonel Dummett died his third daughter Anna, who never married, converted the family home into a lodging establishment in 1845.

21

During this time, Anna ran into financial troubles and her brother-in-law William Hardee stepped in to help out. William was busy with the outbreak of the Civil War by this time. He asked his nephew to help out at the boarding house. While the nephew was there helping out he fell in love with a very beautiful, colored servant girl named Lily (an affection she apparently felt as well). In the 1860s interracial relationships were a huge scandal and the young boy's uncle found out. He could not stand to be shamed by his nephew's actions, so he arranged for him to be sent to military school. Lily's true love refused to be sent away. Tragically, feeling he couldn't live without Lily he went up into the attic and hung himself. The details of Lily's whereabouts after this are somewhat sketchy. She was believed to have continued to work at the inn and was there as late as her early 40s, after that little is known.

The house has continued to function as an inn since Lily's time, and a very popular one at that. The St. Francis is actually considered one of the oldest continually operating inns in America. She has seen much in her history. Many souls have passed through the doors, and some apparently have decided to come back.

Spirits at the St Francis

The most reported spirit at the inn is that of Lily. The apparition of a beautiful woman with a darker complexion and a turban on her head is often seen in what used to be the attic, and most frequently in the room called Lily's Suite. Her spirit loves to interact with woman's personal belongings. Especially purses and make up bags. Could this be because she never had these things as a child? She also frequently likes to mess with the water and make it too hot or cold for unsuspected bathers.

On one occasion, the maintenance men reported seeing a young woman in a white dress wearing a turban going down the back staircase. On another occasion he was going up to Lily's Room to do some repairs and there was a young woman in a white dress wearing a turban making the bed. There wasn't supposed to be anyone there and he went down stairs to ask the girls why there was a housekeeper making up the room (since he was going to be messing things up while making repairs). The ladies looked surprised because there was no one in housekeeping even on the property at that time. They all went upstairs, and no one was there. [During our investigation we got locked out of our room, which was Lily's, twice! Is this a strange coincidence? I don't know, but it has happened to others and the door knobs have been changed out more than once.]

Another room that is active is Elizabeth's Suite. I have heard several different stories about this room. Some say it was named after Colonel Dummett's daughter. Regardless of the origin of the spirit haunting this room, it seems to like to aggravate the male guests. "She" has been known to knock books off the shelf onto the floor in front of them and even touch them with great pressure. This spirit only seems to interact with the male guests, it leaves the ladies alone.

There has been some speculation that perhaps Elizabeth was severely mistreated by a man in life. Whether this is true or not her spirit has been known to frighten several male guests of the hotel who were unprepared for the paranormal activity. More than one of these guests have asked to change rooms or leave all together.

Besides the female spirits, there are a few male resident haunts at the inn. Some people have reported seeing a handsome young man looking very depressed walking around in what used to be the attic (now beautiful guest rooms). Many believe this spirit to be William Hardee's nephew still sad and missing Lily.

A soldier has also been seen by many inn guests and tourists walking by on the corner balcony holding a musket. This spirit acts as if he is still on guard after all these years. He never seems to interact with anyone and clues to his identity are scarce. He may even be from the St. Francis Barracks just down the street which housed the Spanish soldiers in their heyday. I have actually witnessed this ghost for myself in the past. I saw a shadowy figure standing on the balcony. I couldn't make out exactly what he was holding, but it did appear to be something the same size as a musket. A soldier has also been seen standing in the dining room leaning up against the wall.

In addition to Elizabeth, Lily, and the male spirits at the inn, no mention of the St. Francis would be complete without discussing Anne's suite. Anne's suite seems to be the most active room in the entire inn. A female apparition has been seen here and many have reported hearing a female voice, but they can rarely make out what is being said. Guests have reported hearing someone calling their name behind them, only to turn around and discover there is no one there. She likes to randomly move things around in the room as well. One guest reported taking the extra blanket off the bed and setting it on the chair. She woke up the next morning with the blanket spread across her. She was the only one in the room.

In my opinion, The St. Francis Inn is a paranormal melting pot in St. Augustine. Even the St. Francis Park, just across the street, is said to be haunted. As if the inn activity wasn't enough, guests at the inn have reported seeing the apparitions of soldiers at the park as well and they are often reported by guests in the upstairs rooms. While some of the paranormal activity has been frequently encountered by employees, most of the ghostly accounts come from guests. Could this be because the employees are immune to the activity? Or maybe the ghosts want to scare off the help.

It's hard to know everything that may have gone on in this beautiful and cozy inn during the colonial Spanish period, the Civil War and the decades since. These times seem to have left as big of a paranormal mark on the inn as the romantic St. Augustine icon makes on its guests. For a fantastic evening, paranormal or not, this place is an amazing inn and treasured Historic Haunt.

LAUGHNER'S SPIRIT AT THE BEACH DRIVE INN

Beach Drive Inn, St. Petersburg, Florida

I was born in the Tampa/St. Petersburg area. I spent some of my early years there and had heard many stories of haunted places in the area. When I began writing my books I was enthusiastic about including several places from the area in my books. Two of the more noteworthy were the Don Cesar and its ghost-

The Beach Drive Inn

ly ties to major league baseball (which I explored in Historic Haunts of Florida II) and the beautiful Vinoy Hotel (which was included in my first book Historic Haunts of Florida). So of course after a very pleasant and welcoming correspondence I was very excited and only too happy to go investigate the place where the Vinoy's builder, Aymer Vinoy Laughner lived with his wife Stella. Heather and Roland Martinus, the current owners of the Beach Drive Inn (Laughner's former residence), were gracious enough to allow several members of the Historic Haunts Investigation team and I to come down and investigate their historic bed and breakfast. So we made our way down from Jacksonville, Florida.

The bed and breakfast was featured on a cable network paranormal show called Psychic Kids: Children of the Paranormal with Chip Coffey. The show was geared to help children with psychic abilities learn how to deal with what they were experiencing. Chip and the children made contact with some of the bed and breakfast's resident haunts and I had some of the same experiences they did.

A Brief History

The owners believe the house was built in 1910 by Perry Snell (all records before 1913 were destroyed in a fire at the Pinellas County Courthouse).

24

Records do exist from 1914 on and they easily chronicle the comings and goings of this structure's owners. Since 1914 the residence had been bought and occupied by two well known developers in the area, C.R. Hall and William Petten. In 1919, the house was sold again and came under the ownership of Stella and Aymer Vinoy Laughner. According to many versions of the story Mr. Laughner was chipping golf balls in his front yard across the road to an empty lot while he had guests over. Among his guests was Real Estate promoter Gene Eliot. Laughner decided that the empty lot was where he would build a grand hotel. Eliot agreed and wanted to call it the Vinoy 'because that's such a pretty name.' The lot had such a beautiful view they both thought it was the perfect place for a massive hotel. While Mr. Laughner was having the Vinoy built, he had the tall hedges at his home cut down on one side so he could run back and forth to the construction site. Laughner's dream came true when The Vinoy opened December 31st, 1925.

Mr. Laughner enjoyed his vision and his view of the grand hotel from the house until 1961 when he passed away. His wife Stella died in 1976. Their home would change hands several times before being bought in 2006 by the Martinos. In 2007, after some renovations they would reopen the former Laughner residence as the Beach Drive Inn.

The Beach Drive Inn's Ghost Stories

One of the spirits believed to occupy the Inn is Mr. Laughner himself. According to most accounts he was believed to have passed away in the home in 1961. People claim to have seen a gentleman resembling Mr. Laughner here in his old home and across the street at The Vinoy. The owners and staff think that he is responsible for things being moved around or disappearing and reappearing some time later.

The Beach Drive Inn is also thought to be haunted by a female spirit. This spirit is called Mary and is believed to have been a former maid at the residence. She reportedly passed away in one of the rooms (now the Montego Bay Room). Guests have reported seeing the strange imprint of her torso in the mirror and claim she causes furniture to move, especially the antique rocking chair in the room (which was caught on camera in the Psychic Kids episode).

Our Investigation and My Personal Experiences

Our Historic Haunts group pulled out our equipment and began our investigation, but as is sometimes the case, found little to no evidence that night on our meters and with our cameras and EVP recorders. So the Martinos had picked the Montego Bay Room for me for the night and feeling a little discouraged after a very quiet and inactive investigation, I settled in my room. I decided before going to bed to try to contact the spirit who supposedly resided in that room one more time before retiring for the night. The room contained the antique rocking chair in it that according to many guest reports supposedly rocks on its own. I pulled out the flash light and sat it on the nightstand and told Mary, the resident ghost in this room, this was her last chance to talk with me because I was going to bed. I then said, "If you want to talk to turn the flash light on." Immediately after I finished my question the light came on. I asked her if she was attached to the house, but received no response. I asked if she was attached to the chair, and she responded yes by turning the light on.

As I continued with my questions, I asked her if she remember the two teenage girls that came with a camera crew, and Mary responded with yes. Mary had made the rocking chair rock for the girls and they actually captured it on camera. I made the comment out loud that it was kind of creepy for a rocking chair to rock by itself. Coincidentally as I had begun describing the girls and the camera crew I noticed the rocking chair began to rock, but it suddenly stopped as I completed my comment. I thanked her for making it stop. The flash light then came on again. I went on to ask, "Mary, are you the one making things disappear and reappear?" I received no response via the flashlights. I then asked, "Is it Mr. Aymer Vinoy Laughner?" And the flashlight started flicking on and off several times. I then said out loud, "I guess that is a yes!" and laughed. The flashlight once again came on.

By this time it was very late and I was extremely tired. I thanked Mary for talking with me and wished her good night and one last time the light lit up. I went to bed leaving the IR camera running over night hoping to capture some evidence. When I got up the next morning, it seemed that Mr. Laughner had apparently paid me a visit sometime in the night. The camera was turned off, unplugged, and had been moved over about 4 feet from where I had originally placed it. Apparently someone didn't want to be filmed.

The Beach Drive Inn is a peacefully and playfully haunted place to stay while in St. Pete. Whether you come for the ghosts, the panoramic view from the waterfront area, the private roof top sun deck, or the multitude of other amenities; the Beach Drive Inn is guaranteed to offer you a great experience. While you're there make sure you check out the Downtown St. Petersburg Ghost Tour. It is a short walk away and you will hear some amazing ghost stories from this haunted town.

For more info on the inn go to: **http://www.beachdriveinn.com/**
For more information on the tour go to:
http://www.ghosttour.net/stpetersburg.html

THE PLAYFUL AMERICUS SPIRITS
Americus Garden Inn, Americus, Georgia

....

One of Georgia's most celebrated bed and breakfasts is the Americus Garden Inn. This multi award-winning Inn has become a popular haunt of travelers looking for a great place to stay in the region. It has also become a popular haunt for a few playful spirits.

A Brief History of the Inn

The Americus Garden Inn was originally built by James Kelso Daniel in 1847. Unfortunately, he died a short time later in 1851 and left the estate to his wife. She remarried in 1857 to Rev. John Duncan. Their marriage was short lived as she passed away in 1864. The reverend sold the house shortly thereafter.

There were several different owners between 1864 and 1994 when it became a bed and breakfast. Many have speculated the house may have changed hands so many times because of the ghosts that reportedly inhabit this beautiful inn. Others claim it was due to hard times and strenuous upkeep costs for such a grand home.

In 2002 Kim and Susan Egelseer bought the inn. Through their hard work and efforts the site became a top 10 bed and breakfast. They have also received a Traveler's Choice Award along with many other awards.

In 2007 a tornado caused severe damage to the inn and many of the now ancient large trees on the property. The tornado completely devastated the gardens, but not the estate. Since then intensive renovations now have the gardens all looking as lovely as they did in 1847.

Paranormal Reports at the B&B

Owner Susan Egelseer shared some of her own paranormal experiences and that of some of her guests at the inn. Not long after she and Kim had assumed ownership of the bed and breakfast she saw a well groomed Civil War Union solider (appearing to be a general or a man of rank) standing in the balcony suite doorway. He was just staring intently off into the distance. His apparition lingered for a short time before vanishing.

Susan also told me that things disappear all the time and reappear in the strangest places. A room key for example disappeared for months, only to mysteriously reappeared in a trash can of a completely different room. The trash gets emptied every day in every room and a fresh garbage bag is always installed. The ladies thought this was strange, but decided to thank the ghosts anyway for returning the key.

Susan went on to detail some of the experiences of the people who have stayed at the bed and breakfast. Many guests trying to take photos inside the inn wanting to remember their wonderful stay here have problems doing so. When they try to take the pictures their cameras won't work, brand new batteries die immediately, or strange streaks taking up the entire photos suddenly and inexplicably appear. This happens often and taking photos inside the inn seems to be a continued problem.

In addition, the front desk gets phone calls frequently from guests complaining the television in their room changes channels on its own or the alarm clock comes on when it isn't set. Employees and guests alike have caught the scent of what they call "old timey" perfumes of lilac or lavender that seem to suddenly fill the air from out of nowhere and when no one is around. Cold blasts of air are often felt in the dead of winter well away from vents or other air sources when the air conditioning isn't running and the windows are sealed up tight. Sometimes in the summer witnesses have described a gust of air as if someone had just ran past them. Fortunately, running ghosts, cold air blasts and floating perfume scents are unlikely to harm the guests at the Inn.

In fact, there appear to be no malicious spirits at the Americus Garden Inn. I would call whoever they are very playful and curious. It seems that the Union gentleman might have his own company with him here and they all seem to be happy at the inn. Maybe the spirits at the inn are so active because they aren't familiar with all the gadgets and wonderful amenities at the Inn. Perhaps they're experimenting with them and enjoying their time at this lovely B&B. I know I would.

www.americausgardensinn.com

THE CHASE BEGINS AND THE GHOSTS ARE CAUGHT...ON CAMERA

The Kennesaw House, Marrietta, Georgia

The Kennesaw House

Are there ghosts in the greater Atlanta area? Of course. There are no shortage of ghost stories about this amazing city and the surrounding areas. One of the area's more interesting stories involves the Kennesaw House in Marietta Georgia.

The Kennesaw House was built by Mayor John Glover in 1845 in an area that used to be an old stagecoach stop in the 1800's. It is one of the oldest buildings in Marrietta. It was originally built to be a cotton warehouse, but was then turned into The Fletcher House Hotel in 1855 when it was purchased by Dix Fletcher. The Fletcher, as it was known, is where the great locomotive chase began.

The Great Locomotive Chase

During the Civil War, in the early months of 1862, James J. Andrews, a part-time spy and civilian scout, (working with the Union) hatched a daring plot for a military raid in enemy territory. Andrews and a group of men would commandeer a train and take it northward toward Chattanooga Tennessee. Along the way they planned to stop whenever convenient opportunities allowed them to destroy or damage track, bridges, telegraph wires, and track switches behind them. This they hoped, would delay travel on the vital Western and Atlantic Railroad (the W&A) line from Atlanta to Chattanooga. Hopefully, this delay would be long enough to prevent the Confederate forces from quickly moving north and stopping the Union capture of Chattanooga. Andrews recruited civilian William Hunter Campbell and 22 Union soldiers to put the plan into action (these men would later be called Andrews' Raiders). They targeted a locomotive stopping in Big Shanty Georgia (now Kennesaw) because the station had no telegraph and couldn't wire ahead warnings to Confederate forces.

Andrews and his men traveled in civilian disguises and in smaller groups to avoid suspicion. On the night of April 11th, Andrews and some of his men spent the night at the Fletcher House. They woke up the next day on April 12th and from Fletcher House departed to put the plan into effect. Andrews and his men boarded a northbound passenger train along with other passengers which had stopped at Big Shanty. The other passengers, onlookers, crew members, and a number of Confederate soldiers watched in disbelief as Andrews and his men steamed away with the high jacked locomotive The General and the first several rail cars.

The angry and determined conductor of the train William Allen Fuller gave chase with two other men, first on foot and later by hand car. Because of hilly terrain to the north of Atlanta; The General never got up to great speeds. The terrain and Andrews' periodic stops to sabotage meant Fuller stayed hot on his heels. Fuller commandeered two different locomotives to pursue before he ran into destroyed tracks courtesy of Andrews' efforts. Fuller continued on foot before taking command of the locomotive Texas, a southbound train in Adairsville. To continue pursuit he had to run the locomotive backwards!

Andrews continued his movement and the Union forces (thinking ahead) had cut the telegraph lines to prevent word of his theft from spreading. However, his luck took a turn for the worse when rain soaked wood prevented burning bridges and other acts of destruction. Eventually, The General would run out of fuel in Ringgold Georgia, eighteen miles from Chattanooga. Andrews and his Raiders left The General and scattered, but they were all caught in short order. Many were hung (including Andrews). Private Jacob

Wilson Parrott was awarded the first Medal of Honor for his part by Secretary of War Edwin Stanton. The General would find a home in the Southern Museum of Civil War and Locomotive History in Kennesaw Georgia.

The Kennesaw House After the Great Chase

General Sherman and the Union forces would march into Atlanta in 1864. The Kennesaw House was one of the only buildings in Marrietta to not be burned by William Tecumseh Sherman's Atlanta Campaign. Partly because Fletcher was a Free Mason and his son in law was a Union Spy. Sherman would briefly use The Kennesaw House as his headquarters. It would later serve as a make shift hospital and morgue during the war. After the war it would serve as a site for retail shops and an office complex. It was renovated in 1979 with a restaurant in the lower floor. Since then the building has been restored and is now the Marrietta Museum of History, with a gift shop, staff offices and exhibits, community space for events, and storage.

Seven Hundred Plus Ghosts?

The publicized paranormal activity at The Kennesaw House has drawn many paranormal groups as well as features on CNN, PBS, and the History Channel. It reportedly hosts over 700 ghosts! While this amount seems a little fanciful, and maybe due to the large number of men who may have been treated or died at the former Fletcher House Hotel, there are several reports that are frequently repeated.

James Andrew's spirit is said to still be roaming the halls of this historic building. Many people report hearing the tapping sound of a ring along the hand rail of the staircase. Perhaps James is still planning his theft of the locomotive.

People have also seen medical procedures taking place. The scene suddenly, takes place right before them, as they turn a corner or come into a room. It disappears just as quickly as it appeared. This seems to be residual energy imprinted here from when the building was used as a Civil War hospital.

In addition to historical and surgical apparitions, a man around 5 feet 7 inches tall has been seen as well. He appears to be a Civil War era doctor and many refer to him as the doctor or doc. He is believed by some to be an apparition of Dix Fletcher's nephew, who was a Union soldier and surgeon.

A female apparition has also been seen at Kennesaw House and has even been captured several times on security cameras (which have since been removed by the facility). In most of the descriptions her hair is pinned back and she is wearing a light colored dress. Some people have reportedly been touched by her. She often appears to visiting children, who claim she resem-

31

bles the paintings of Mrs. Fletcher on the Kennesaw walls.

Besides these very specific apparitions, there are several other odd phenomenon experienced at Kennesaw House by staff and visitors alike. Unexplained noises, footsteps, and the smell of cigar smoke are often reported. Further, the elevator has been known to frequently and inexplicably go to the top floor by itself and open its doors (perhaps to let out unseen or non-living residents) before closing its doors and returning on its own to the basement.

Now that this building is a historical museum, it is full of antiques and artifacts. Who knows who or what might be attached to the items on display in this old building. One thing most who have experienced paranormal phenomenon here agree on is that there is nothing at the museum that is malicious. Everything seems to be peaceful and content. There is no negative energy in this Historic Haunt, just some amazing exhibits of a difficult time in America's past.

SPIRITS BREWING AT MOON RIVER
Moon River Brewery, Savannah Georgia

Savannah has long been one of my favorite cities. Besides the romantic draw of this beautiful southern gem; it has also long been a draw for those interested in the paranormal. Savannah is one of a handful of cities that can stake a claim to the title of most haunted in America (New Orleans, Charleston, and St. Augustine rank among its notable southern contenders). Even among this haunted Georgia locale there are stand outs. Moon River Brewing is considered by many not just a great historic site and popular restaurant and brewery; it is also thought by many to be Savannah's most haunted location.

History Brewing at Moon River

The Moon River Brewery was once known as the City Hotel. It was built by Charlestonian Elazer Early in 1821 and was the first hotel in Savannah. It was also home to the first branch of the United States Post Office in Savannah. It has hosted a variety of well-known guests such as the Marquis de Lafayette and James Audubon.

The City Hotel would serve double-duty on multiple occasions providing a make shift hospital during several yellow fever outbreaks. Savannah and the hotel would survive these outbreaks, but several hundred people would perish in the process. Unfortunately, many died at the City Hotel and many of them were children.

In 1851, Peter Wiltberger bought the City Hotel. He would make many renovations and stop at nothing to help drum up business. At one time he even housed a live lion and lioness at the hotel in efforts to gain publicity and notoriety. Despite Wiltberger's efforts the final guest at the hotel was in 1864 just days before Union General Tecumseh Sherman marched through during the Civil War.

In the aftermath of the War Between the States, over the next few decades, the former hotel would serve as a lumber and coal warehouse, business offices, and more until 1979 when Hurricane Dave went through and blew the roof off part of the building. The building sat empty and in a state of disrepair until 1995. During that year the former City Hotel would enjoy some changes and a short existence as the Oglethorpe Brewing Company until 1999. In 1999 further renovations took place and the Moon River Brewery opened to the public.

Violent Acts Leave Lingering Paranormal Impressions?

Throughout the building's history, a few violent and notable acts took place. Most of these occurred during its time as a hotel. In the spring of 1832, an argument broke out between an unpopular local, James Jones Stark, and Savannah doctor Phillip Minis. Stark was known to be something of a troublemaker and braggart and reportedly became a sore loser after Minis beat him during a night of gambling. Stark would spend the next several months bad-mouthing the reputable Savannah doctor to all who

33

would listen. By August, Stark was still throwing slanderous words around about the doctor and apparently one day while in the hotel bar would pay the price. Though details of the account would vary, most describe similar scenarios involving Dr. Minis. The good doctor reportedly walked in, pulled a gun, and shot Stark on the spot. Later, while on trial, Dr. Minis swore Stark had tried to pull a gun and that was why he had shot him. The doctor was acquitted and the town was glad to see Stark dead.

Another violent and notable occurrence at the hotel happened in 1860 when New Yorker, James Sinclair came to town and stayed at the hotel. The southerners of Savannah didn't seem to like him very much. In fact they tried to run the "Yankee" out of town. Sinclair refused to leave and the town formed an angry lynch mob. They dragged him into the streets and practically beat him to death.

Many Spirits Found at the Brewery

The Stark and Sinclair incidents might help explain why the spirits here aren't always the friendliest. Many guests and employees report getting; slapped, pushed, and hit at Moon River Brewery. Moon River staff have also described other paranormal incidents including bottles being thrown, rattling glasses, silverware inexplicably sliding across surfaces and doors slamming shut.

In the 1990's during renovations, the foreman's wife got violently pushed down the stairs by one of the entities residing in the building. It is said the foreman quit that day. The upper floors still remain empty today.

One "resident" spirit often encountered is known as "Toby" and he seems to stay in the area of the billiard room. Many guests have reported being pushed or touched in that room by this entity. Toby's spirit has been encountered by Moon River employees as well.

Another bit of paranormal phenomenon encountered at the Brewery occurs on the upper floors. A glowing white apparition is often seen there and is believed to be a former employee of the hotel who died here in the late 1800's. This entity has been nicknamed "The Lady in White" and has been encountered by many. She is described as wearing 1800s style garb while moving through the restaurant or stairs to the upper floors. Her apparition has been reported by a multitude of witnesses as she apparently goes about her business before vanishing into thin air.

The basement area at Moon River Brewing is often used for parties and large gatherings and looks very much like a dungeon. This might help explain the frequent paranormal activity in the basement. People have reported shadow figures in this area along with cold spots and drafts that seem to come out of nowhere.

Still it is the recurring and sometimes violent paranormal activity at this building that has drawn several ghost hunting groups and caused it to be a popular subject of nationally televised paranormal shows. Even without the tv specials, being a fairly frequent visitor to Savannah, I am very familiar with the Moon River Brewery. So familiar that on Saturday, July 14th, 2012 my husband (knowing of my interest in the place) got down on one knee and asked me to marry him after claiming I needed to see the activity on the K2 meter (the ring was underneath). As a result I have to admit, it is one of my favorite Historic Haunts in Savannah.

ARRR THERE PIRATE GHOSTS HERE ....OF COURSE

The Pirate's House Restaurant, Savannah GA

The Pirate's House

Avast ye scurvy landlubbers! One of Savannah's most popular spots for locals, privateers and tourists alike is the Pirate House. Many of the restaurant's patrons (myself included) find the lure of a rich history and a wealth of tasty menu options to be too much of a treasure to pass up. Over the years I've spirited away many friends and family members to this haunted locale to share great grub and ghostly tales.

Of Past Times and Pirates

What Savannah residents now know as the Pirate House Restaurant was originally located on the site that was once known as Trustee's Gardens. It was America's first experimental garden, and was named after General Oglethorpe's men, who traveled with him from England, in 1733 to settle the city of Savannah. Botanists were sent to procure plants and see what would thrive in the new land. Cotton and peach trees did quite well and became a major commercial crop for the colonists.

The small building now adjoining The Pirate House was built in 1734 by the

35

colonists as the gardener's house and is said to be the oldest building in the state of Georgia. It is now known as the Herb House and is constructed of bricks which were made along the banks of the Savannah River. You can actually dine inside this tiny building once you enter the main building of the Pirate's House. Speaking of the main building, the main portions of the restaurant were built in the 1750s along with an inn which was badly needed for all the seamen coming into the important trade port of Savannah.

In a short period of time, what started as a simple inn and restaurant became well known and popular with sailors and blood-thirsty pirates. Despite the fact that sailors and pirates loved to drink here they weren't exactly the best clientele the inn could have. While they were there heavy drinking was rampant and all sorts of roguish behavior was all too common.

Stories of the Pirate House's Infamous Past

The main portions of the restaurant today, known as the Captain's Room and the Treasure Room, have a very old world nautical feel (much as they did back then). The walls are adorned with old pirate maps, wooden beams, and portraits of old ships. While today's patrons might feel that it has a charming feel to it, it was only a few centuries ago that pirates made their plans to shanghai unsuspecting sailors and their ships here. The Old Rum Cellar found beneath the Captain's Room was the topic of many stories that described tunnels running to the shore. It was also here where pirates would drug sailors, take them to their ships and make then join their cause or die. In some cases the sailors would wake up from being drugged or knocked out at sea on an unknown ship. Here they found themselves members of a new crew whether they liked it or not.

Some stories even claim that many parts of the famed book, Treasure Island, were based on factual events. It has been further suggested that they took place here at The Pirate's House. Many believe that "Captain Flint" died in one of the upstairs rooms.

Pirate House Progresses

Mrs. Hansell Hillyer took over the buildings that make up The Pirate's House Restaurant in the 1940s and turned the place into what it is today. Not only can you come here and have a fabulous southern meal, you can also roam the rooms and buildings that make up this amazing Savannah landmark. When you step through the front door it's as though you have entered another time. With 15 separate dining rooms there are plenty of places for patrons to sit and spirits to hide. In fact, the Pirate's House is said to be one of Savannah's most haunted buildings.

The Pirate's Paranormal "Crew"

Captain Flint is believed by many to be one of the ghosts still haunting this historic gem. Many claim to have seen the pirate captain on moonless nights. Not only is Captain Flint or someone resembling him seen but other piratical apparitions have

Arrr There Pirate Ghosts Here...of Course

been seen and heard as well. More than one member of the wait staff has witnessed an apparition sitting at a table with a mug of grog. This sailor appears so real witnesses are convinced it's a living person, until he disappears right before their eyes.

Some visitors that have ventured in to the Old Rum Cellar have been disappointed to see the tunnels that once ran to the river are now all bricked up. However, some of these same witnesses are suddenly excited to see apparitions of what appear to be two pirates escorting an unconscious man straight through the wall! According to most reports this frequently occurring phenomenon is followed by an icy cold blast as the apparitions vanish.

These types of pirate apparitions have been witnessed by many. Even though the tunnels have long been bricked, it is still evident where they used to be. Residual energy still seems to be haunting the cellar as the pirates are still walking through with their unsuspecting victims.

This is just a taste of the variety of paranormal activity recurring at the restaurant. Even if you don't have a ghostly experience at The Pirate's House Restaurant, it is still worth a visit. As a major piece of Savannah's history, with amazing food to boot, this Georgia landmark is a spot worth setting sail for.

THE GHOST OF JESSE JAMES
Old Talbott Tavern, Bardstown Kentucky

Old Talbott Tavern

Kentucky, the so called "Bluegrass State", is known by most for the Kentucky Derby, Kentucky Fried Chicken, the Mammoth Caves, and Fort Knox. To those who dig deeper Kentucky is known as the state where the first cheeseburger was served in 1934, where Corvettes and Post-It Notes ™ are manufactured, and where Daniel Boone is buried. Kentucky also has several haunted hot spots, one of the more interesting is Old Talbott Tavern.

Kings, Coaches, Gunfighters, and Ghosts

The Old Talbott Tavern was built in 1779 and is known as the oldest western stagecoach stop in America. The location of the tavern was perfect as it was situated near the end of the stage coach road that led east to Virginia and Pennsylvania. Most stagecoaches stopped here for room and board and to rest the horses before continuing on.

A variety of statesmen, soldiers, explorers, and even exiled King Louis Phillippe have stayed here. There are murals on the walls (uncovered in 1927) believed to have been painted by Phillipe or someone in his entourage. Within the murals are bullet holes found in the walls believed to have been left by Jesse James or his cousin former Sheriff Donnie Pence. One of them reportedly had a little too much to drink and thought he saw the birds or butterflies in the murals move so he shot at them. As if that wasn't enough, one of our greatest former presidents Abraham Lincoln even stayed here as a child with his parents.

The Old Talbott has been continuously operating since it was built (except closing for a time to repair fire damage). This makes it not only one of the oldest bars in America, but also reportedly the world's oldest bourbon bar. The tavern has gone through a variety of owners and name changes, it was once known as the Hynes Hotel and later the Newman House. In 1886 George Talbott bought the tavern and was married soon after. Talbott and his wife Annie would have twelve children, six of which died in the tavern. Talbott himself died in the tavern in 1912 prompting his widow to change the name from Newman House to the Old Talbott Tavern. In 1916 the tavern was sold to T.R. Beam (Jim Beam's brother). Beam later sold the bar to bourbon distiller Tom Moore. Moore ran the tavern from his purchase of it in 1926 until 1964. It has been sold several times since and survived a terrible fire in 1998 that destroyed the roof and most of the second floor. It was during this time that the tavern closed briefly to perform repairs and reopened in 1999 (unfortunately the murals were damaged and have yet to be fully restored). With this kind of background it is no surprise that the tavern might also serve up a few more ethereal spirits.

Spirits and Occurrences at the Old Talbott

Paranormal occurrences happen on such a regular basis at the Old Talbott that the employees don't pay it much attention anymore unless it is something extreme. Among the frequently reported occurrences are silverware moving, objects being relocated, and keys disappearing from the front desk only to reappear elsewhere later in the day. Other more unusual reports detail furniture that starts "jumping up and down", round orbs of colored light that hover over beds and move around in mid air, and a phantom child that "spoons" with sleeping guests in the General Quarters room (so named because Revolutionary War hero General George Rogers and General George S. Patton have both stayed here). People have also frequently reported seeing shadow figures, hearing voices, hearing phantom footsteps, doors suddenly opening and closing, in an otherwise empty tavern, as well as seeing full body apparitions.

In fact, apparitions have been seen many times simultaneously by more than one witness. When more than one person or witnesses experiences this type of apparition it is called a collective sighting. Understandably this usually makes the sighting seem more valid than if an individual person was the only one to have witnessed something. On at least one occasion a group saw a male apparition and followed him to see where he went. The apparition headed down the hallway where the witnesses watched him walk through a locked door. Many have encountered this apparition. Some believe this is the ghost of Jesse James. The details of the apparition and the witnesses descriptions bare an uncanny resemblance to photos of the former visitor James. Some suggest his spirit may be returning to visit his cousin, former sheriff Donnie Pence.

The other entity frequently encountered here is known as the lady in white. She has been seen in a long flowing 1800s style dress making her way through various parts of the house. In most reports she simply hovers over people then just floats away.

KENTUCKY

Many believe her to be the spirit of former owner and care taker Annie Talbott.

With the frequency of paranormal activity encountered at the Old Talbott Tavern its no wonder guests have sometimes been known to check out in the middle of the night due to the paranormal activity going on in their rooms. This landmark tavern was once even touted as the 13th most haunted inn in the U.S. Whether you are drawn here as a bar fan, by the ghostly activity, or by the place's amazing connection to bourbon, you are sure to enjoy this Revolutionary era gem and Historic Haunt.

SPIRITS AND BOURBON
Bourbon Orleans, New Orleans Louisiana

New Orleans in the 1800s was a true melting pot of culture and diversity. The city and its culture were influenced heavily by its population of French, Creole, Spanish, American and colored descent. One of the buildings that was at the heart of these cultural movements and the French Quarter itself (the Vieux Carré) was the Bourbon Orleans.

photo courtesy of Bourbon Orleans

Details of the Bourbon

The Bourbon Orleans is located directly behind the St. Louis Cathedral. The hotel is composed of four buildings; the Orleans Ballroom which was built in 1817, a red brick building from the late 1800s, a U Shaped building from 1960s (which surrounds the pool courtyard), and a small cottage with a courtyard. In the early 1800s The Orleans Ballroom was connected to the Orleans Theatre. The theatre was destroyed by fire in 1816, but the ballroom survived and was finished by 1817. The theatre was rebuilt in 1819 and it burned again in 1866. Yet again, the ballroom survived.

Grand balls, galas, and other events were often held at the Ball Room and when joined to the adjacent Orleans Theater were called "Gala Nights". In 1825, the grandest balls of all were given for the Nobleman Marquis de Lafayette. The Orleans Ballroom was considered by many the most beautiful in America. Interestingly enough it would come to be named for a rather unsavory local practice and not the Gala Nights.

The Quadroon Balls

It was commonly known as the "Quadroom Ballroom" a place where wealthy white men of means would attend after the theatre looking for a young eligible woman who was one quarter African. These women were called "quadroons" and

41

were typically the offspring of a mulatto and a white person. The quadroon balls were extremely popular and only people of certain social rank could afford to attend. The women were by all accounts lovely, refined and fashionably dressed. The men were seeking what some called a diversion with courtesans, but what was known locally as a left handed marriage or "plasage". The women who agreed (and most had few other options) had "arrangements" made with their parents to be kept in a furnished home with finances provided for her and any children. Should the white suitors choose to end the arrangement or marry a "proper" white woman, the quadroon would keep a financial settlement and find other means of support. These types of balls and the practice died out before the Civil War.

By 1881 the structure was no longer used as a ballroom and was sold to the Second Order of African American Nuns, The Sisters of the Holy Family. St. Mary's Academy was founded by the sisters in the 1850s and they moved into the much needed space in the 1960s. In 1964 the ballroom building was bought by a local developer and turned into the Bourbon Orleans Hotel. The Ballroom underwent a renovation in 1984 to restore it to its former glory, and the entire property underwent a restoration project to the tune of 15-million dollars. The current Bourbon Orleans is now an updated reflection of its former self, but many of the spirits from its past are still here.

The many spirits of the Bourbon

One well known spirit here at the Bourbon Orleans is known as the "Ballroom Dancer". She has been seen dancing throughout the ballroom to mysterious music. She often appears in a misty or transparent form with long raven black hair dancing to the waltz being played by an unseen orchestra.

Breaking the Habit

When the nuns took over, they built a chapel in the area that was once the ballroom. They inscribed above the ballroom doorway, "Silence, my soul; God is here." Maybe they were hoping this would cleanse the atmosphere from all the wrong doings that once took place.

Despite their best efforts to avoid the unpleasantness of the area there is another apparition that is often seen and is known as the "Suicide Nun". Stories claim that the nun took her own life in the chapel room, but not one seems to want to verify it today and the nuns won't discuss it. There have been several reports describing the apparition of a woman in a long black robe wearing a habit. Maybe she feels she cannot pass on since she committed what they believe is the "one unforgivable sin". During their time here the sisters took care of the poor, the elderly, the sick, and the orphaned. Room 644 often has guests complaining of hearing mysterious cries and seeing the apparition of a nun in their room just watching them.

The Confederate Ghost

Female spirits are not the only ghosts encountered here. There is also a wounded soldier who is often seen. He is wearing a Civil War Confederate soldiers uniform and seen walking the halls or standing at attention and reaching out for help. He appears to have a bleeding wound that looks so real people get very concerned when they see him. Witnesses confuse him with a seriously injured living person. Apparently, he never received a proper burial and that, perhaps is why he is still here. Witnesses also claim to hear mysterious footsteps and what many believe is the disembodied sound of a sword dragging across the marble floors.

Children's Ghosts

During the Yellow Fever epidemic many of the children being cared for died and never left. The spirits of many of these children are apparently still here (especially in the lobby and kitchens). People have reported cold spots, heard laughter, or have felt a small hand touch them. A little girl is often seen running around as well, sometimes chasing a ball. Servers at the hotel claim to frequently see the motion of table skirts and glasses when the children's spirits are heard.

Investigating the Bourbon

This is another investigation we are looking forward to during our next New Orleans trip in 2015. We have the investigation scheduled and will post details on our website about our findings at www.historic-haunts.net The Bourbon Orleans has a history of paranormal activity and we hope to experience some of it when investigate for ourselves.

ETHEREAL LADIES OF THE EVENING

Dauphine Orleans & The Audubon Cottages, New Orleans, LA

Dauphine Orleans

New Orleans has always had a colorful history, especially in its "Red Light District". In the early 1830s, Basin Street was the bustling main artery of life for this active region of town. The street was full of pretentious and luxuriously expensive brothels ($25-$50 a night). In these dens of delight champagne flowed freely, ladies wore evening gowns, and musicians, dancers, and singers were abundant. Eventually by the 1870s Basin Street was overwhelmed and the surrounding areas (including Dauphine Street) began to see ten dollar "parlor houses", fifteen cent "cribs", and everything in between pop up. An Alderman named Sidney Story tried to halt the spread of prostitution by proposing it be legalized and restricted to a certain area. Ironically, much to his dismay, the area became known as the Storyville district and became New Orlean's most rollicking neighborhood. Licensed and under the control of the New Orleans City Council these "houses" were pulsing with life. Palatial Mansions had their own orchestras (which counted among them some of the most historic American Jazz musicians), cabarets, dance halls, and luxurious French Quarter "cottages" and all thrived with the vibrant and exciting energy of the region. Among these lively places were the Dauphine Orleans (May Baily's place back then) and the Audubon Cottages.

44

May's Place

May Baily's Place was known as one of the better bordellos or "sporting houses" in New Orleans. The place was built in 1821. It was located in the bustling red light district of Storyville.

May Baily and her younger sister Millie were children of Irish immigrants who passed in 1847 during the yellow fever epidemic. The sisters went into the brothel life to make their own money and to do as they wished. May was the Madam and Millie was one of her girls.

During these heady days of the Storyville district and its legal brothels, the place now known as the Dauphine Orleans, was licensed to May Bailey as a house of prostitution for the ladies under the "Ordinance Concerning Lewd and Abandoned Women". Even now, when you check into the Dauphine, you receive a copy of the license issued in 1857. The original one is hanging in the lounge. While in operation May's place gained a reputation and like much of Storyville saw ladies and vice come and go. Through it all May and Millie supported each other and kept the place going.

While Millie was here "working" for her sister, she met a Confederate soldier, El Dorado Ark, in 1861. She fell madly in love with him and he proposed to her even though he disapproved of her line of work. Millie started planning their wedding and picked out her dress, but the wedding never took place. Her fiancé was shot dead during a gambling dispute on the morning of their wedding. May helped Millie through the tough time and their place, like Storyville, continued to thrive until World War I.

By 1917, the Department of the Navy decided as a matter of National Security that a "make war not love" policy was best. At their insistence the bordellos, stand alone cottages, and sporting houses were shut down. The government was concerned that disease would spread to the service men shipping out of New Orleans to fight in Europe. This area of New Orleans would continue to host a lively nightlife, but the days of that type of high paid and excessive hedonism would never reach the same levels. The owners of the places adjusted as they could and the city moved on.

Today the Dauphine Orleans, formerly May Baily's place, has benefitted from multi-million dollar renovations and offers modern amenities while proudly displaying the opulence of the Storyville era. In fact, a red light still burns in the hotel's courtyard next to May Baily's Place. If this colorful history and the hotel's proximity to Bourbon Street aren't enough to draw your interest, perhaps the fact that its also haunted might.

Dauphine's Spirits

One of the ghosts that haunts this historic location is Millie. At the time friends closest to her claim that after her fiancé died she kind of lost her mind. She was never the same after receiving word of her husband-to-be's death and started wearing her wedding dress around the sporting house. Many Dauphine Orlean's guests and employees have reported seeing her apparition roaming the property in a white wedding dress. She is most often seen in the courtyard and walking down the hallways. She is also seen on the balcony, possibly still waiting for her fiancé to come back to her. She is often referred to as the "Lost Bride".

Another spirit seen at the Dauphine is of a little girl named Jewel. She is known as

45

the "Dancing Girl" and appears to be between the ages of 12 and 15. She is seen dancing throughout the hotel and courtyard and seems to be very happy. Jewel has been reported occasionally ethereally traveling with a ghost cat. Many people and guests have reported seeing and feeling something furry rub against their leg, but when they look down, nothing is there.

Other stories of the Dauphine and its haunted residents include reports of the apparitions of long gone ladies of the evening, and a mysterious black gentleman named George. There's even a ghost in white who apparently likes to knock the books off the shelves in May Baily's library.

The Audubon Cottages

Just behind the Dauphine Orleans is the Audubon Cottages where activity of the paranormal is also no stranger. Named after naturalist painter John James Audubon, these seven private and historic cottages were built shortly after two great fires destroyed most of the city in the late 18th century. They surround what is thought to be the oldest pool in the French Quarter. Cottage one is where the painter completed his birds of America series, but each cottage has its own unique history and stories. Cottages number two and four are particularly active to this day, at least in the paranormal sense.

The apparition of a country music loving Confederate soldier is often seen on the balcony of Room #4. Could this be Millie's betrothed returning for his bride? Or could it be another soldier arriving to visit the girls? A General is also seen in the area of the Audubon Cottages as well. Many suggest he is there trying to discourage his soldiers from visiting the house of ill repute and keep his men focused.

New Orleans (and her many hotels, cottages, and buildings) is an amazing and lively place. My group Historic Haunts Investigations and I are hoping to investigate here next summer. Perhaps some of the resident haunts will visit us upon our arrival so we can tell more of their stories, and gather more evidence for fans and skeptics alike. Regardless of whether you come for normal or paranormal reasons, the Dauphine Orleans and the Audubon Cottages are amazing and historic musts if you are traveling to the Crescent City.

*Sample of
A License for
Loose Morality*

*Courtesy of
Dauphine Orleans*

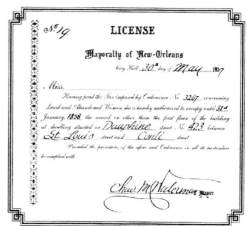

THE SPIRITED FRENCH PIRATE

Lafitte's Blacksmith Shop Bar, New Orleans LA

Lafitte's Blacksmith Shop

Beads, beads, beads! Mardi Gras and beads are often the first things that jump to many people's minds when they think of New Orleans. The French Quarter and Bourbon Street in particular have long held a place of fame during this decadent time of year. However, what is often overlooked by festival-goers and tourists in their efforts to grab hurricanes and other drinks in places like Pat O'Brien's, is the rich history of another Bourbon Street staple, Lafitte's Blacksmith Shop.

The Colorful History of Lafitte's

The building now known as Lafitte's Blacksmith Shop and Bar was thought to have been built prior to 1772. Some attribute the structure to a building project by Nicolas Touze sometime between 1722 and 1732. It is one of the few places in America that can lay claim to be the oldest continually occupied bar in the U.S. This New Orleans landmark has survived through two of New Orleans great fires at the turn of the 19th century (1788 and 1794) that burned much of the French Quarter. The building's survival may have been due to the building being constructed with a slate roof, which may have saved it from the worst of the fires.

Between 1772 and 1791 it is believed that the Lafitte brothers, Jean and Pierre, used the property for the New Orleans base of their smuggling operations. They set up Lafitte's Blacksmith Shop as a front. This according to the details of the property owned by the Duroche family (a.k.a. Castillon) and Privateer Captain Rene Beluche.

Captain Beluche commanded his own ship the "Spy" which was in Lafitte's Batarian fleet. Lafitte and his brother Pierre over several years had enjoyed great suc-

47

cess "privateering". They raided foreign ships and stole their cargos which they later smuggled into New Orleans and sold. However, when the U.S. passed the Embargo Act in 1807, the Lafitte's moved their operations and fleet to Bataria Bay, Louisiana. They continued to have success moving smuggled goods into New Orleans.

Throughout these years as the Lafitte's were in New Orleans and pirating, they both made enemies. Especially the dashingly handsome and notorious ladies man Jean. He reportedly had MANY mistresses, but only one true love. She was the wife of the then governor of the Louisiana Territory. It is believed they were eventually found out. Afterwards of course, the governor and the New Orleans government began to snoop around the Lafitte's operations.

American naval forces entered the Batarian area in September 1814 capturing most of Lafitte's fleet in the process. With his brother and men still imprisoned Jean Lafitte arranged bail. While out on bail Lafitte was approached by British officers who offered him a British Navy position if he helped them attack New Orleans. Instead, the crafty Frenchman worked out a deal to free his brother and men after contacting the U.S. forces. They helped General Andrew Jackson defend New Orleans in early 1815 against the invading British and earned themselves legal pardons for their past smuggling efforts. Lafitte and his brother would later become spies for Spain during the Mexican War of Independence, moving to Galveston Island Texas in the process. From here he continued to pirate and attack merchant ships until his mysterious death in 1823. He left behind a rogue's legacy and one of the most haunted bars in the French Quarter.

Reports of Paranormal Activity at Lafitte's

There have been many reports by witnesses who describe seeing a dashing gentleman on the first floor near the fireplace who suddenly disappears right before guest's eyes. Lafitte's ghost has even been seen at the bar or at a table having a beer. Lafitte's apparition has also been spotted in the ladies room. No surprise perhaps since he was a big fan of beautiful woman.

The fireplace on the first floor (where Lafitte reportedly hid his cashes of gold) seems to have a lot of activity around it. Besides Lafitte's ghost being seen in the area, patrons have also reported being touched by an icy cold hand while positioned nearby. Others have reported feeling like someone is in the dark shadows of the bar watching them and have even described glowing red eyes. Many employees even refuse to close the bar alone because of these encounters and the spooky ambiance of the bar itself.

Besides Lafitte, another ghostly apparition often described in paranormal accounts is that of a female. She is most often encountered on the second floor. She is often seen as a reflection in a mirror. Details about her possible origin are a mystery, but judging by most accounts describing her appearance and wardrobe she is definitely from a different time.

While it is sometimes hard to separate legend from fact in the Crescent City; Lafitte's is a city icon. Located a mere two or three blocks from the rowdy center of Bourbon Street the structure has survived fires, hurricanes, and other incidents that have made it a New Orleans and French/Cajun legend. It is definitely worth checking out while in New Orleans, paranormal fan or not!

THE PHANTOM OF THE OPERA HOUSE

Grand Opera House, Meridian, Mississippi

"Opera is where a guy gets stabbed in the back, and instead of dying, he sings."
—Robert Benchley

A humorous quote about an art form loved by some and loathed by others. Besides Opera, the ornate buildings that housed performances would also showcase drama, comedy, theatre and dance performed by traveling shows, vaudeville groups, theatrical troupes and many others. Before the advent of motion pictures, Opera houses provided the only venues for many communities to experience culture and entertainment.

One of these communities was Meridian, Mississippi. Much of the town was destroyed during Sherman's March South in the Civil War. However, Meridian, unlike other parts of Mississippi, would have several things working in its favor in the rebuilding era following the war. First, it was ideally positioned where the Mobile and Ohio Railroad, and the Southern Railway of Mississippi converged. Second, it was the most logical stop via rail between New Orleans and Chicago. As Meridian began to rebuild and grow into one of Mississippi's largest cities, developers and entrepreneurs took notice.

Meridian's Historic Lady

In 1889, a group of entrepreneurs formed a partnership. The group consisted of Israel Marks and his brothers; Levi, Sam, and Marx Rothenberg. They decided to expand their retail operations by opening a swanky new wholesale and retail mercantile store in Meridian. They were also going to add an adjoining hotel.

The site they chose covered a ? block (which equaled 5 lots) facing 5th Street and 3 lots covering 22nd Avenue and 6th Street. During their research and construction they decided against the hotel and opted for an opera house. Commercial space with leased shops would occupy the first floor and would provide additional income. The opera house would involve less overhead and be much more profitable than the hotel. The Marks-Rothenberg partnership spared no expense; they hired J.B. McElfatrick, a veteran designer of over 200 other theatres in the U.S. The opera house would include over 1000 seats with a stage 30 feet wide by 50 feet deep (easily accommodating lavish shows from New York).

Above the stage was a 35 foot high arched proscenium with an ornate painted border that featured a beautiful woman in the art work. She was positioned there as if she were overseeing everything going on at the opera house. She was referred to affectionately as "The Lady", and became a symbol of the Opera House.

The Grand Opera House was completed in 1890 and opened in December with Johann Strauss in "The Gypsy Baron". During its heyday the Grand Opera House enjoyed mostly packed houses. It drew big name performers the likes of Sarah Bernhardt, Helen Hayes, and Henrik Ibsen (performing ironically in this case in a play called "Ghosts"). The Opera House went through renovations in 1902, moving the entrance and adding electricity.

49

As the craze of Motion Pictures swept America, the opera house was renovated again and partially converted into a movie theatre with a large silver screen. The gallery was divided into two areas to allow for projection of the films. The Opera House owners leased the building in 1923 to Saenger Theatres who ended up fighting them over the right to modify the building again. Saenger lost in 1927, but with the Great Depression hitting in 1928, the company leasing the building filed for bankruptcy, shortly thereafter Levi Rothenberg died and the doors were locked on the historic Grand Opera House.

A Rebirth of Sorts

Fast forward to 1988, the Grand Opera House was donated to the Historic Meridian Foundation. They were delighted to discover that the theatre, sealed as it was all those years, remained virtually unchanged since it closed 60 years earlier. Efforts to collect donations and restore the Opera House and adjacent storefront began. On March 11th, 1993 the site was designated the Official State Opera House of Mississippi. After painstaking fundraising and renovation efforts -to the tune of $25 million dollars - the building that once housed African American companies, minstrels, vaudevillians, and silent movies, was fully restored and reopened as the MSU Riley Center, The adjacent department store was converted into a state of the art conference facility and both buildings provide space for classrooms, rehearsal halls, and studios to people from college to kindergarten.

The Grand Opera's Phantom

Apparently, someone from the Opera House's past is still residing here. This beautifully restored gem sometimes experiences disembodied singing ringing through the rafters. Employees closing or cleaning late at night will hear a beautiful woman's voice coming from the stage as if she were warming up before a performance. A female apparition has also reportedly been seen in a wispy form gliding across the stage. No one seems to know who she is they just assume she's a former performer from the theatre's heyday. This entity is sometimes referred to as "The Lady" in reference to the painted image above the stage.

In addition, theater-goers and employees have reported abnormal cold spots and feeling hands touch their shoulders. None of the paranormal incidents reported would indicate anything evil or malicious. In fact, the performers in the theater often describe feeling and experiencing sudden "positive vibes" that they weren't feeling prior just before they prepare to go onstage. Perhaps they are experiencing the energies of this historic opera house and its own lady phantom.

THE ENCHANTED ANNABELLES
Annabelle Bed & Breakfast, Vicksburg Mississippi

Overlooking the Mississippi River in Vicksburg is the Annabelle Bed and Breakfast. This Victorian era favorite features an amazing main resident's house and a guest house overlooking a fifty-five foot long gallery. The main house was built in 1868 and the guesthouse was built in 1881. The main house was built by John Alexander Klein on his cedar grove estate for his son Madison and is located in the Historic Garden District. There have been several reports of paranormal activity in the Garden District, but with many frequently involving the Annabelle, it's no wonder this B & B is a popular spot for investigators.

Enchantment at the Inn

The inn has been investigated on numerous occasions because of the many reports of the "enchantment" at the inn. One of the teams that went in recently set up their equipment, as all investigation groups do, hoping to catch proof of the paranormal. They weren't disappointed. Cameras and digital recorders confirmed that there is a presence in the Rose Room. Spirit orbs were captured on video on the staircase and in the parlor area.

In addition to the activity in the Rose Room, other rooms at the inn also seem to contain paranormal energies. The Dixie Room reportedly has recurring visits from the spirit of a one-legged Confederate soldier. The Annabelle's activity is not just limited to these two rooms. Many reports described similar details encountered by several guests throughout the former residence.

Many people have reported feeling a cold chill, even during the hottest Mississippi summer months. There have also been numerous reports of the sudden and strong scent of perfume. Other reports mention the smell of medicine which fills the air as if you were in a doctor's office. Neither of these phantom scents can be described away by guests, candles, potpouri or other obvious culprits.

Owners of the inn and investigators believe there is a female spirit present because of the perfume scent. While this female entity seems to spook people, apparently its unintentional. Among the other activity attributed to her is phenomenon involving the television. The television has been known to cut off or change channels of its own accord. Perhaps she just doesn't like what the guests are watching.

Whatever you experience any of the commonly reported incidents from the ghostly house guests ,you are sure to have a charming stay at the Annabelle. As a former winner of Best B&B in the South and more recently voted among the top 2% of B&B's in the U.S., there's no doubt the Annabelle will be serving up her best. Just remember as you soak up the opulence and victorian era flavor that you might not be alone. There might be a little haunt with your hospitality.

GHOSTLY RESIDENTS OF THE BILTMORE

Biltmore Estate, Asheville, North Carolina

The Biltmore Estate

The first time I visited the Biltmore Estate I was on a sixth grade field trip. During my first visit here I really didn't know much about it except that it was built by George Washington Vanderbilt II and it was an amazing estate. We thought the place was amazing. How many families have a library, indoor swimming pool, and a bowling alley inside their home? We thought it was the coolest thing we had ever seen, we "ooo'ed" and "ah'd" the entire time. As we approached the bottom of the staircase leading to the third floor the tour guide stopped and explained that there were more rooms up there. I asked the guide, "Who is he?" and pointed upstairs. The guide turned around and looked up the staircase then turned back to me and asked in a hushed voice, "Do you see him?" I smiled and nodded. The guide looked a little spooked and quietly whispered, "We aren't supposed to talk about it" then led us in the opposite direction of the staircase. Little did I know just how much history the place had and that there were haunts attached to it.

Building the Biltmore

George Washington Vanderbilt II made regular visits to Asheville North Carolina during the 1880s. He loved the beauty and clean air of the mountains and the wonderful summer climate. He decided to build his summer house here and construction began in 1889. His summer home was completed by 1895 and was a MODEST (?) 175,000 square foot mansion with 250 rooms. Among my favorites are a gorgeous two story library, indoor pool, bowling alley, and a multitude of bedrooms. Biltmore also housed some 19th century novelties like an intercom system, fire alarms, forced air heating, and elevators.

After Vanderbilt's death in 1914 he left this massive estate to his widow Edith and their only child. Edith followed through with her husband's wish and aided the somewhat depleted Vanderbilt fortune by selling 85,000 of the 125,000 acres they owned to the US Government. This land would remained mostly untouched and would become the heart of the Pisgah National Forest.

In 1930, the Vanderbilt's only child, Cornelia Stuyvesant Vanderbilt and her husband opened the house trying to bolster the estate's financial situation during the era of the depression. The family continued to live in the house until the 1950s when it was permanently opened as a house museum to guests from around the globe. During WWII the Biltmore even housed paintings and sculptures from the National Gallery of Art in Washington DC to protect them in the event of an attack on the Capitol.

Today the Biltmore is the largest privately owned home in the US. In fact, it is still owned by a Vanderbilt descendent, grandson William A. V. Cecil. The entire estate consists of approximately 8000 acres. You will find original furnishings and Vanderbilt artifacts throughout the estate and even on the grounds. In addition to the house you can tour the winery, horse barn, farm, and Antler Hill Village, but let's get to the hauntingly good part.

Biltmore's Haunts

Many believe George Washington Vanderbilt is still here in spirit. They theorize that because he lived in his home a very short period of time after its competition and didn't have time to fully enjoy its grandeur he's come back. Others believe his spirit is here because he wants to care for his home and family still to this day. If so he may even be trying to figure out who all the intruders are in his home. According to many paranormal reports George is often seen and felt in the library. His apparition has often been seen sitting in one the chairs reading one of the books from his extensive collection. Coincidentally, his appearances seem to occur most often when storms roll through the mountains.

In addition to George there are reports of two other female entities. One is believed to be Edith. People have claimed to hear Edith softly talking, possibly to George. Many witnesses have described a wispy woman walking through the house before disappearing. Many think the descriptions match Edith's.

There is also said to be a woman in black heard crying throughout the halls. Some speculate that this could also be Edith, a residual haunt morning the loss of her husband, but others say the apparition's appearance marks it as a completely different entity.

My Experiences and Investigations

Another experience I had here as a child was on that same school trip and consists of phenomenon commonly reported by witnesses. During the trip we were walking through the amazing pool room and several of the kids (myself among them) swore we heard splashing and saw wet foot prints. Some of the kids in our group even mentioned hearing disembodied laughter. We pointed it out to our teacher and she said it was all part of the tour. A few years later when I returned on another visit, the footprints were not there. I asked this guide about the reports of the pool room and the disembodied laughter and was told it was not part of the tour. Then the male guide said, quietly, "It was the ghosts!" After talking with him for a few minutes I learned there is a ghostly pool party that occurs often and has been reported frequently. He also shared with me that in the billiard room sometimes people have reported the sound of balls "breaking" on the pool table as if a game was getting under way and the smell of phantom cigar smoke. He said they really weren't supposed to talk about those things but he was quitting in a couple of days and moving out of state so it didn't matter and then he laughed.

After hearing from this guide I started speaking with many more people at the estate, and people who have visited there. I soon learned that there have been and incredible number of paranormal encounters, way more than I thought. What makes the reports of unusual phenomenon even more appealing is that they span a large group of demographics. Most of these witnesses were unfamiliar with the details of activity at the estate, but reported strikingly similar details in their accounts.

I am very much looking forward to returning here. Perhaps, I can investigate with my team someday. I recommend the place to paranormal fans or just interested tourists. Whether you experience the ghosts here at the Biltmore Estate or not it is an amazing piece of America's Historic Haunts.

GROVE PARK'S FRIENDLY PINK LADY
Grove Park Inn, Asheville, North Carolina

The Unique Grove Park Inn

Nestled in the hills of Asheville North Carolina is one of the most unusual and beautiful hotels in America, The Grove Park Inn. While its unusual appearance tends to catch the eye of visitors from a distance; it is full of other features that make it even more distinct. This Blue Ridge Mountain beauty is an AAA, 4-Diamond Resort (since 2001). It is also considered one of the top resort spas and gold and tennis resort in the US (Conde Naste and Travel and Leisure). It also boasts several distinguished culinary award winning restaurants and the terraces are an amazing place to watch the sunset or hold an event. If all of this wasn't enough, this immense (55,000 square feet) an amazing hotel can claim not only one of the best and most hospitable staffs in the south, it can also claim its own friendly ghost.

Grove Park's Beginnings

Edwin W. Grove the so called "father of modern Asheville" was born in 1850 in Tennessee. After serving in the Civil War, he hatched a plan to pursue a career in pharmaceuticals. While still in his 20s he purchased Paris Medicine Company, based in Paris, Tennessee (it was later moved to St. Louis). E.W. Grove would soon make his fortune in pharmaceutical development. His most well-known medicine was Grove's Tasteless Chill Tonic (a tasty syrup elixir containing quinine). The tonic was said to take care of the chills brought on by malaria and other maladies. It was so popular by the late 1890s that it had become a household staple and outsold Coca Cola! Grove first visited Asheville North Carolina because of respiratory problems he was having. At the time, Asheville was known for its clear air thought to aid the body.

55

Grove ended up building a summer home here.

In the course of pursing new pharmaceutical inventions, Grove met and befriended Fred Seely in Detroit (another man striving to make a name for himself in the pharmaceutical business). Grove invited Seely to his summer home and eventually Seely went to work for him. While staying with Grove, Seely met and fell in love with Grove's daughter Evelyn and married her.

In 1909 E.W. Grove bought 448 acres of land to build a grand hotel to attract people for the health benefits and ideal location. He loved the design of the Old Faithful Inn and Canyon Hotel in Yellowstone National Park and took many of their features for his new hotel. With the help of his friend and son in-law Seely, Grove began construction on this arts and crafts style resort. Seely gave his word that the inn would be open in a year or less.

To accomplish this feat hundreds of granite stones and tons of supplies were carried up the mountain for the new hotel. Horse and wagons were used for bringing supplies to the construction site. At the time, four hundred men were working on the inn, and doing ten hour shifts six days a week. To help expedite the building the men were paid the handsome sum of $1 per day and they stayed in circus tents on site.

When The Grove Park Inn opened in 1913 (11 months and 27 days later) it had 150 rooms. The hotel would enjoy great success and gain an impressive reputation. During WWII it functioned as an internment center for Axis diplomats, a rest and rehabilitation center for returning Navy sailors, and an Army redistribution station. The Philippine Government even function on the grounds in exile during the war from the Presidential Cottage. A decade after the war (1955) the inn became part of Sammons Enterprises under the direction of Mr. and Mrs. Sammons. They expanded it greatly and now this grand hotel has 512 rooms total.

The hotel has fairly recently become part of the Omni hotel chain, but is no less amazing. Over the years a variety of famous politicians and note worthies have stayed here. Among these are ten presidents, entertainers Will Rogers, George Gershwin, and Harry Houdini, and authors and inventors like F. Scott Fitzgerald, and Thomas Edison. In some cases these stays are marked by plagues on the doors that make these rooms well known. One room in particular is very well known and known to be very haunted. The room is on the fifth floor of the main and original part of the hotel, its room 545.

Grove Park's Ghostly Activity

Room 545 is known as the Pink Lady's room. I have been fortunate enough to investigate here more than once and I have to admit the fifth floor and room 545 in particular have a feel completely different than the rest of the hotel. The reasons for the rooms activity and Pink Lady's exact origin is something of a mystery part local lore and part speculation.

The Story of the Pink Lady

In the 1920s a beautiful young woman by the name of Helen was reportedly staying in room 545. Helen was believed to be an unlucky debutant or an eager participant in an alleged affair with a married man. Most stories differ as to whether she slipped and fell or was pushed to her death just outside her room and over the ledge. Clad in a beautiful pink gown she fell to the Palm Court atrium just a few floors down breaking her neck and dying instantly.

Many believe she is still here seeking justice and wanting truth to be known on what really happened to her. Others believe she may be just residual energy drawn to all the granite in the hotel and the mountain. Granite is known to hold energy and many believe this is why her energy is so strong.

"The Pink Lady" as she has come to be named (because she is most often reported in a pink gown or manifesting as a pink mist) has been seen and felt at the inn for nearly 100 years! She has been known to act kindly to guests, pulling the covers up, playing with hair, and even holding hands. On one occasion a doctor left a note thanking the hotel for the pink lady who played all day with his kids. This entity is known to love children and manifests to them more frequently than adults. She's also something of a prankster, reportedly tickling toes and feet, closing and opening doors, and turning lights, ac units, and electrical devices on or off.

I spoke to a friend and former employee at the Grove Park Inn. He claims to have witnessed a misty apparition in the hallway of the fifth floor just outside of the Pink Lady's room. He said it didn't interact with him, it just floated down the hall towards the door of room 545, then vanished into it.

I also spoke with a guest who frequents The Grove Park Inn and always stays in the original portion of the hotel. She refuses to stay in room 545! She said she and her family love the fifth floor because of the views, but one night while staying in 545 they were woken up by the spirit of The Pink Lady at 2 a.m. That was enough for them.

One time while visiting here at Christmas time for the Gingerbread Competition we went up to the fifth floor to pay our respects to the ghost and we ran into a housekeeper. She said she wouldn't clean that room alone. The first time she went in there she claims she had heard the stories, but chose to ignore them. She had left the door open while she was changing the sheets and the door suddenly slammed shut. That was enough for her and she hasn't cleaned the room alone since. (This was several years ago and I do not know if she is still working there).

Retro Image with carriage courtesy of the Grove Park Inn

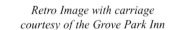

My Investigations and Thoughts

During my investigations of the Grove Park Inn and room 545 cold spots have been felt every time and major temperature fluctuations of more than ten degrees. We also experienced spikes with the K2 EMF meter during these rapid and unusual temperature changes. After discounting leaking windows, air ducts, and other possibly explanations for unusual activity in the room, it's hard to ignore the fact that something unusual seems to be going on there.

The Pink Lady's ghost is not malicious, but does tend to spook people who don't know about her. She has been described as a kindly spirit and most at the inn seem to enjoy her being there. For some (especially paranormal fans) she is as much a draw perhaps as the inns, other amazing features. If you get a chance to visit the Grove Park you will find that the spa is magnificent, the food is amazing, and the golf is reportedly spectacular (I don't play). There are also two amazing stone fireplaces in the lobby and old elevators positioned interestingly within the stone walls. Visitors will discover the place still has the original feel that Mr. Grove gave it when it originally opened in 1913. I encourage you to visit near the winter holidays when the decorations and events like the Gingerbread Competition really make the place a standout.

The Grove Park Inn is one of my favorite Historic Haunts in Western North Carolina and I can't wait to go back.

THE HAUNTED HAMMOCK
Hammock House, Beaufort, North Carolina

North Carolina is a vary diverse state where I spent some of my childhood. Visitors to the state can easily go from beach extremes like the Outer Banks, to river rafting, hiking in the mountains, or watching race car driving among other things. The variety in the state is reflected in the cities, their history and in the legends, lore and even ghost stories. One of the more interesting to me has always been Hammock House in Beaufort.

A brief look at the Hammock

The two story white house in Beaufort North Carolina that is known as the "Hammock House" was built around 1700. The reason its called the "Hammock House" is because it is built on a hammock, "a fertile raised area" of land. It was most likely originally built as an inn due to its location on the inlet overlooking the Atlantic Ocean. Besides the house being an inn it has also served as a school, residence for Union soldiers, and a private residence.
Stories floating around Beaufort claim that the building is very haunted and that this explains why it has had at least 30 different owners since it was built!

The Hammock's Haunts

One of the more fearsome ghost stories attached to this building is connected to one of the most dreaded pirates of all time, Blackbeard. Apparently, Blackbeard stayed here for a short time with one of his 13 wives. Before Blackbeard went back out to sea and left the Hammock House he had his current wife hung from one of the Oak trees on the property. There have been many reports of paranormal incidents on nights when the moon is full and shinning down on this sleepy town. Apparently in many of these incidents the blood curdling screams of Blackbeard's hanging wife can still be heard.
In addition, people have also reported seeing Blackbeard's ghost ship off the coast as well. Could he still be seeking treasure in the town or searching for the thirteenth wife that outlived him?
Another apparition seen at the Hammock House is said to be Richard Russell Jr. Russell reportedly returned to Beaufort in 1747 from a long excursion at sea and was furious with one of his slaves. He climbed the steps into the attic of the house with his slave so he could "punish him". However, the slave outsmarted or overpowered Russell and broke free. He pushed his master to the bottom of the steps. Russell apparently died from a broken neck and the slave fled. His spirit has been encountered at the Hammock on numerous occasions.
The third ghost most often encountered on property can be traced to the Civil War. In March of 1862 the town of Beaufort found themselves under the control of the Union Army. Three Union officers found the (at the time) abandoned Hammock

House and decided they could use the house as their quarters. After they entered the house the three officers were never seen again. Or were they? In 1915 during renovations to the back porch the remains of the three men were discovered. Witnesses claim to have seen the apparitions of three men in Union blue uniforms on the property. Perhaps these unfortunate men fell victim to the other spirits of the house.

Many claim that even though the beautiful Hammock House has been masterfully restored, the efforts for a new look stirred up old ghosts. There are spirits which paranormal incidents would suggest still reside here and actively draw attention to themselves. It is truly an amazing Historic Haunts of Beaufort and tells a twisted tale of tragedy and loss. I hope to inspect this unique house for myself, hopefully I'll have better luck than the Union soldiers.

LATTA GHOSTS
Latta Plantation, Huntersville, North Carolina

Location! Location! Location! A common mantra in real estate and an important decision in the early days of America, especially, when choosing a site for homesteading. In 1797, farmer Moses Hayes selected 100 acres of land in Mecklenburg County - property which had changed hands several times before - and decided to homestead on it. Hayes would make some improvements including the building of a log cabin, before selling the property in 1799 to a Scot named James Latta.

Latta Plantation

The Latta Era

Latta was believed to have come to America from Ireland in 1785 to settle his father's estate. A widower with two sons (William and Robert), James Latta noticed a ripe business opportunity for he and his sons as "merchant". He found great success traveling to Philadelphia and Charleston purchasing goods he would later sell to Carolina farmers and villagers from the back of his Conestoga Wagon. There was a great demand for his products as his customers sought everything from common items like needles, salt, sugar, toothbrushes, cooking tins and pots, to the rarer commodities like bridle bits, fine silks, and china. The growing populations of these areas and their growing demand for items made this peddler very successful.

James would marry again in 1796, this time choosing a local girl named Jane Knox from nearby Lincoln County. By this time his eldest son William was already on his own and his youngest Robert was showing promise as a young man following in his father's merchant footsteps. In 1800, James built a Federal style home for his second wife believed to be based on houses he noticed while doing business in Philadelphia. Latta would buy more land in 1813, 1816 and 1817, eventually owning over 700 acres. As he grew older, the strong entrepreneurial spirit Latta possessed would cause him to move away from the merchant business and into establishing a cotton plantation. His eldest son Robert would assume responsibility for the mercantile business, moving to Yorkville, South Carolina, and eventually buying out his father's interests. Robert would become the wealthiest man in South Carolina. Meanwhile, James and Jane Latta while establishing a thriving cotton plantation would have 4 children. They had three very beautiful daughters and a son named Ezekiel (the youngest). Unfortunately, Ezekiel was sickly and died at the early age of ten at the Plantation.

The Latta's suffered through the grief of their son's death, and concentrated on mak-

61

ing a good life for their daughters on a successful plantation. The large acreage they owned and utilized for cotton growing required a large number of hands to assist. The Latta's were slave owners and at one point had a total of 34. The slaves were the main reason the plantation thrived the way it did. James died at the plantation in 1837 at 82 years old and his wife remained on the property until she moved in 1839. James, Jane, and the children are all buried just down the road at Hopewell Presbyterian Church.

The Plantation Changes Hands

David Harry purchased the house and 420 acres of property in 1841 from Rufus Reid, Latta's son-in-law. The property wouldn't stay with the Harry family long. After David's passing, his heirs sold it to William Sample in 1853. Sample's family would control the plantation and grounds throughout the Civil War era and beyond (one of Sample's sons even served in the Confederate Army). In 1922, the tract of land was deeded to Southern Power by the Samples family and after a merger in 1927, Duke Power obtained the property. They in turn, donated three acres of land and the homestead to Latta Place, Inc. a non-profit organization. In 1975, the property was listed on the National Register of Historic Places. That same year the house and land were deeded to Mecklenburg County. Today the property (and additional acreage purchased by the county) houses the living history museum, hosting 12,000-20,000 school children per year. The county has also added trails, an equestrian center, a honey bee exhibit, a bird sanctuary, and the Carolina Raptor Center. The plantation has become an informative and popular place for adults and children throughout the county and surrounding area.

Latta Paranormal

The stories told to adults and children visiting the plantation may be more than just historical. There are quite a few interesting ghostly tales attached to Latta Plantation. Reports abound from staff and visitors describing ghostly children running and giggling in the attic. The strange thing is there are no floor boards up there for anyone to being walking on. Perhaps there used to be a proper floor, and maybe the children used to sneak up there to play? Other reports detailing activity involving children describe feeling a presence in the children's bedrooms. Interestingly enough, an inexplicable swarm of ladybugs in the hundreds have been reported on the ceiling of the kid's room as well.

Kids and ladybugs aren't the only occurrences described in the paranormal accounts of the homestead. People have reported being touched in the main house. In several reports people have felt a cold hand on their face. One gentleman even reported someone grabbing his shirt collar from behind him and tugging on it. He turned around to see who was there and found an empty room.

There also seems to be some incidents of paranormal activity involving objects in the former homestead. When employees arrive in the morning to prepare the building to open for guests, they have at times found a mirror lying face down on the floor. The first time this occurred the employee thought an antique piece had fallen off the wall and broken. But, when the mirror was examined it wasn't broken and it was much too far away from where it was hanging on the wall to have fallen off and landed in that location. This incident has occurred several times and the mirror has never even been chipped. Besides the mirror, other eyewitnesses have described a walking cane in the house that moves on its own. Even more unusual, many people have reported the intense smell of apple pie baking, when the kitchen is not in use, and no air fresheners or candles are present.

As for the grounds around the house, some say that James Latta is still heard and seen on the property. They report seeing a well-dressed man in period clothing walking the grounds as if he is still examining things and making sure everything is running to his specifications. Other paranormal accounts describe a man with mutton sideburns running up the front steps. Perhaps the Latta family never left, or maybe they've just returned to their old Historic Haunt.

BLACKBEARD'S GHOST SHIP
Ocracoke Inlet, North Carolina

Ocracoke Inlet

In the 1700s most people knew of and feared the nastiest pirate ever known to man, Blackbeard! Described as an angry man full of rage, he had little concern or sympathy for anyone or anything. He sailed the seas hunting for treasure and didn't care who he stole it from or where it came from.

The description alone of Blackbeard was enough to terrify people. He wore his beard long in braids, and lit slow burning matches which he placed within the braids. This made him look even more intimidating and hellish as if he burned outside with the same hate that consumed him inside. Further intensifying his look was the fact that the matches created an appearance in which he was surrounded by smoke. He always kept 6 pistols loaded and ready to fire on a strap across his chest, and sported a variety of daggers, swords, and other weapons hidden all over his body. With this kind of fearsome presence and reputation it makes you wonder how he could have been married 13 times before his death (unless they were all too terrified to turn him down or he gave them no choice).

Blackbeard's Demise

In 1718, the British Royal Navy and Lt. Robert Maynard arrived hoping to put a stop to Blackbeard. They took a fleet of ships out into Ocracoke Inlet where they knew Blackbeard loved to sail on his ship, the Queen Anne's Revenge. On a bloody day in November they got the best of the pirate, but it took 20 bullets and a beheading to finally take the pirate down! Many reports claimed that even after his head was sliced off, the evil pirate's headless body still swam around the ship several times before vanishing into the water.

The Business of Blackbeard

Many restaurants and stores in the village of Ocracoke and ships in the harbor have named their businesses or boats after the famed pirate. Blackbeard's legend is still drawing tourists and very much alive in the region. Many believe that Blackbeard is still sailing along the inlet, possibly searching for treasure....or maybe his head!

Getting There

To get to Ocracoke Island you have to take a ferry boat and once you arrive it has a very secluded feel. Besides having the oldest lighthouse on the east coast (1823) it also had an area known as the graveyard of the Atlantic. This area is just a short distance from the coast where many ships went down before the lighthouse was built. These vessels were victims of terrible storms and the jagged coastline until the lighthouse was constructed.

Ocracoke's Ghosts

There is one ship in particular that many have reported seeing to this day. That ship is the Queen Anne's Revenge, a vessel that sank close to 300 years ago! On stormy or overcast days there have been hundreds of reports by witnesses who claimed to have seen a misty grand masted ship sailing off the coast flying Blackbeard's well know flag, the Jolly Roger. Just as quickly as these witnesses saw it, they claim it vanished. Some witnesses even reported capturing photos of it.

Exploring Ocracoke for Myself

While visiting Ocracoke and sailing across the inlet I couldn't help but notice there was a different feel to this area. I was born and raised in and on the water, I am also a scuba diver so I feel completely at ease on the water. However, sailing across Ocracoke Sound it felt as if there was someone unseen out there watching us.

The entire time on the water we were constantly watching the horizon and all around us it was as if we were expecting to suddenly see a ship come upon us. It was a very rattling sensation as if we were in tune with the same sense of foreboding the other seamen must have experienced when they saw the Queen Anne's Revenge approaching. Only later while in the village of Ocracoke did we find out about the ghost ship frequently seen off the coast and in the inlet.

If you are going to visit Ocracoke make sure to take your camera with you. Besides the beautiful and quaint village that deserves to be photographed, you never know when that ghostly ship might appear right before you. I hope to come back soon and interview more witnesses and perhaps experience the ethereal boat myself. What a fascinating Historic Haunt.

GHOSTS IN THE GARDEN

Magnolia Plantation, Charleston, SC

The Magnolia Plantation House

There are a lot of plantations in the south. Many with striking similarities in look and purpose. Magnolia Plantation is not one of these typical plantations. Considered Charleston's most visited plantation; it is known as the oldest public tourist site in the low country and the oldest public gardens in America. If that wasn't enough to distinguish it from its contemporaries, the Audubon Swamp Garden on site boasts an unmatched natural gathering of alligators, otters, turtles, and birds. All of these features help draw a huge number of visitors every year. Once you learn this gorgeous locale is also haunted it comes as no surprise that it draws paranormal investigators and history buffs as well.

Magnolia's Past

The beautiful Magnolia Plantation has been in the same family since 1679. In that year Thomas and Ann Drayton moved to Charles Towne from Barbados and built their plantation along the Ashley River. They would be the first in a direct line of ownership that would last some 300 years (and continues to this day).

The Drayton family primarily earned their money from the cultivation of their rice crop, a very profitable commodity. However, Magnolia Plantation's operations would be disrupted for a time during the Revolutionary War as it would experience both British and American troop occupation. Drayton's sons fought vigorously against British rule as both statesmen and soldiers.

When Thomas Drayton (the great grandson of the original Thomas) died in 1825 it was his desire to keep the property in the family. Unfortunately, with no male heirs, he decided to leave the plantation to his grandsons (his daughter's children) Thomas and John Gimke. This inheritance was hinged on the promise that the boys took their mother's maiden name of Drayton. Both boys did so and John Gimke Drayton moved to England and began studying the ministry while his brother Thomas Gimke Drayton stayed on at the plantation.

While John was in England he received word that his older brother had died on the steps of the plantation of a gunshot wound (incurred during a deer hunt). As the custom of the time was for the oldest male heir to inherit everything, John had most likely figured while he would be taken care of he would never inherit anything with his older brother first in line. He was of course quite surprised to find himself a wealthy man upon his brother's death. He came back to the states and at the age of 22, was the new master of Magnolia Plantation.

After returning to America, mourning his brother, and spending some time at the plantation, John pursued a career in the ministry and moved to New York. While he was there he met and married Julia Ewing, daughter of a prominent Philadelphia attorney. He brought his new bride back to Charleston to live at the plantation and continued his clerical studies. Trying to manage a plantation, and continue his work with the church all did a number on his health.

He caught tuberculosis, but unlike most that contracted it, he survived, claiming that his cure for the illness was working in the gardens. He built the spectacular gardens for his wife so she felt at home and would forget Philadelphia and any desire to return there. Eventually after his health improved, he became rector of Saint Andrews Church. He continued to care and develop the gardens until his death.

The War of the States and Beyond

The Civil War took a toll on the family and the plantation, but unlike many other plantations they survived and recovered. After the war was over, the gardens and plantation thrived and grew better than ever. In fact, the gardens became so beautiful and well known that the family opened them to the public in 1870. Revenue from the gardens actually helped the family survive and thrive even more.

The family continues to thrive after all these years. The plantation is still in the Drayton family. While the area has gained notoriety for the plantation and gardens, it has also become known as a haunted location. Apparently, many of Drayton family members long gone are still here in spirit.

Magnolia Plantation's Ghosts

Some of the ghostly encounters witnesses describe involve the apparitions of a man and a woman quietly walking through the gardens. Many speculate that this could be Julia and John still enjoying the beauty of what he created for her. Others witnesses have reported the apparition of a man on the steps of the plantation home. Some believe this could be Thomas still falling to his death from that fatal gunshot he suffered during the hunting trip?

A popular paranormal tv show filmed an episode here. They claimed they heard a little girl's voice and an adult woman, but couldn't make out what was being said. They also investigated reports describing the sounds of music playing, a common element in many paranormal accounts of the place and its activity.

Historic Haunts Investigates

While I was here in 2012 and touring the grounds I went to check out the gift shop. All of a sudden I had that "I'm not alone" feeling. I turned to look around and saw no one there. I went over to the counter to make a purchase and asked the attendant, "So, who haunts this place?" The lady acknowledged the truth in my question, but smiled before replying, "I don't talk about that sort of thing."

Another common report on the grounds is of a growling sound being heard. I heard no such sounds here while I visited, but had some thoughts on this. After touring the property and noting its location on the river and the few ponds on the grounds, I noticed there were several alligators swimming around. Alligators do growl and can be very loud. Perhaps the people who had heard the growling sound, and aren't familiar with this beautiful reptile had mistaken it for something paranormal.

I encourage everyone to make a trip to explore Magnolia Plantation. Come here and enjoy the place in all its glory; the gardens, the house, the river, the alligators, and the history. You can spend an entire day at this amazing Low Country Historic Haunt, and perhaps a member of the Drayton family may come back to join you

GHOSTS ALONG THE BATTERY

Two Meeting Street Inn, Charleston, South Carolina

Two Meeting Street Inn

As a paranormal investigator I am blessed that many gracious folks allow me to come research and investigate their locations. Many of these locations pique my interests and stay with me. One such place was Two Meeting Street in Charleston South Carolina.

The Spell of Two Meeting Street

My husband Deric and I were invited to the Inn in Charleston, South Carolina in January of 2013. Owner Jean Spell wanted us to hear the history and ghostly tales of her haunted bed and breakfast. We even had the opportunity to conduct a mini investigation of this beautiful historic inn.

According to Mrs. Spell the inn was built in the 1890s by Martha Williams and Waring Carrington. The two built the structure after their wedding in 1890 upon receiving a generous wedding gift from Martha's father. The gift was a check for $75,000, which was an astounding amount at the time and to this day. Martha's father, George Williams, was a very wealthy Charleston merchant who owned a grand mansion just down the street from where the newlyweds would create their home.

In 1946 the grand mansion became an inn when Minnie Spell Carr purchased the property. It is now owned by Minnie's youngest nephew Peter Spell and his wife Jean

69

and their two daughters. It is a popular Charleston Inn and according to Mrs. Spell, is very haunted.

Tales of the Paranormal at Two Meeting Street

Jean shared some of the frequently reported paranormal encounters on and around the property. Many guests staying at Two Meeting Street have seen ladies from the mid to late 1800s just across the street at White Point Gardens. According to many witnesses it appears as if they are having afternoon tea and are chatting up a storm on the latest happenings in Charleston. Guests have never been able to make out what is being said but it sounds like a grand conversation filled with laughter. They seem to be residual energy because they've never interacted with anyone else and the phenomenon replays on a frequent basis.

Another ghostly sighting of note has been spotted by people leisurely passing by the inn or visitors to White Point. These reports detail the apparition of a Confederate soldier or possibly a General sitting on the front porch. The spirit disappears as quickly as people report seeing him. There is speculation that this entity could be attached to the house that was originally here before the Carrington's built their home.

Besides the frequent reports of paranormal activity on the outside of the inn and the nearby regions, unusual activity has been reported within Two Meeting Street as well. One of the experiences guests have had at the inn is caused by the clock on the second floor. It has been known to chime at 2am, this despite the fact that the clock doesn't work! Its actually missing parts to make it chime. In fact, my husband and I also experienced this phenomenon during our night at the inn, the clock was just outside of our room in the hall. At 2 am, I was awoken by the clock chiming.

Surviving Misfortune

When Hurricane Hugo hit in 1989 it did over $500,000 in damage. It collapsed the third floor granite chimney and a waterfall came flooding down the staircase to the first floor. In addition, all the windows on the first floor were blown out. It's only because of diligent restoration efforts that visitors to the inn today would be hard pressed to find any trace. The restoration has been executed so beautifully you feel like you are stepping back in time into a grand southern manor house. This restoration might help explain the more recent rash of paranormal activity at the Inn as this type of activity seems to stir the supernatural.

A Final Note for Paranormal Fans

Two Meeting Street Inn makes an amazing haunted home base for exploration of Charleston's more spirited sites. If you want to learn more about the paranormal, in town I recommend you check out one of the Bulldog Tours. You can take paranormal tours of the Old Jail, the Provost Dungeon, (and actually go inside the buildings) or take a haunted tour of the cemeteries in town. Charleston is considered one of America's most haunted cities, and I consider Two Meeting Street Inn a special and beautiful Historic Haunt.

www.twomeetingstreet.com
www.bulldogtours.com

RED LIGHT SPIRITS

USCGC Comanche, Off Charleston's Coast South Carolina

There are many tales of the fine large warships and carriers that served our country during WWII. However, what is a little harder to find are details of the other support ships that thanklessly performed their duties and sometimes get lost in the shuffle. The United States Coast Guard's Comanche was one of these ships and had an interesting life and perhaps an even more interesting afterlife.

The Story of Comanche

The USCGC Comanche was built by Pusey and Jones Corporation in September 1934. She was commissioned on December 1st, 1934 for Coast Guard duty before WWII. She was part of the South Greenland Patrol before she was transferred to the Navy on July 1st, 1941. During the war she was extensively used for convoy operations to Greenland and other activities.

The Comanche was 165 feet long and weighed over 1000 tons. She was capable of breaking ice two feet thick because of her reinforcements. During her WWI military time she escorted lightship #110 to Portland Main and participated in many ice breaking activities. The Comanche was also used for helping with supplies when not breaking ice or escorting convoys.

On January 29th, 1943 the Comanche began escorting convoy SG19, consisting of SS Dorchester, SS Biscaya, and SS Lutz for Greenland. In the early morning hours of February 3rd, 1943 a German submarine, U223, fired five torpedoes at the convoy with the Dorchester being hit the hardest at 1:02 am. The Comanche tried to protect the convoy and rescue the men from the Dorchester with an enemy sub still in the water, but they had their work cut out for them.

In the arctic north, the Coast Guard and others would typically use red lights on the life-saving flotation devices instead of the standard white. This was so they would stand out among the white ice and snow. The Comanche did everything they could to rescue all the survivors, but the Dorchester went down in about 20 minutes. The Comanche's crew searched tirelessly for red lights on the life vests and boats to save the men. The Comanche was only able to rescue a total of 97, the Dorchester went down so fast that nothing could be done for many of the others. Another ship, the Escabana, came in to try and help and was able to save an additional 132, but many lives were still lost that morning. The Dorchester was believed to have had a total of 150 crew members and 850 Army passengers.

Despite that dreadful morning, the Comanche continued her war efforts. She was still in service breaking ice and escorting other boats through the hostile waters throughout the war and for a time afterwards.. She was decommissioned on July 29th, 1947.

In 1984, the Virginia Pilots Association donated the Comanche to Patriots Point and she was on display until September 1989 when Hurricane Hugo came through. The winds and waves from the hurricane slammed the Comanche into the side of the

71

neighboring USS Yorktown. This did little damage to the Yorktown, but badly damaged the Comanche.

In 1991 a difficult decision was made, since the cost of restoration was too high, the Comanche would be scuttled. She was hauled several miles off the coast of Charleston and sank to create an artificial reef. The Comanche may have gone to a watery grave, but the ghost stories started when she was docked at Patriots Point, and possibly before.

The Haunted Red Light District

The still anchored USS Yorktown allows Boy and Girl Scouts to camp out on the ship from time to time. One night, while the Comanche was still on display at Patriots Point, a young boy got away from his group and was found on the Yorktown top deck staring down at the Comanche. One of his troop leaders came over, worried the boy might fall off the deck of the ship. When he arrived he realized what the boy was looking at. The scout and troop leader both saw red glowing balls of light off the sides of the Comanche apparently floating in the water. As quickly as the two saw them, the lights vanished. They went and shared their stories with the staff who work aboard the USS Yorktown. They had apparently seen them before as well.

Even today with the Comanche being an active reef, the phenomenon continues. Despite the fact that the Comanche rests approximately twelve miles off the coast, people in boats and out on the water frequently report seeing red glowing balls of light in the location where the ship was sunk.

Could the crew still be looking to be rescued? Or could this just be residual energy from that tragic day attached to the ship? I remember seeing the Comanche as a young girl and for some reason I didn't want to go aboard because I felt nauseous. I experience this periodically and suddenly at certain haunted locations, although at the time I was too young to know it. Perhaps I was picking up on the unfortunate energies of this submerged Historic Haunt that still serves our country.

THE SPIRITED YORKTOWN
USS Yorktown, Patriot's Point, Charleston, South Carolina

The Yortown docked at Patriot's Point

Charleston, South Carolina has many interesting areas to explore. One of these areas is Patriot's Point. Nestled here along Charleston's waterways is the massive and impressive vessel the USS Yorktown. She has had several unique things happen in her long history that distinguish her from her peers. For me one of the more interesting is the fact that she is haunted. Falls is haunted!

The Carrier's Past

The aircraft carrier, the USS Yorktown, took a little over a year to construct and was sent into WWII on April 15th, 1943. The USS Yorktown was named after the Battle of Yorktown which occurred during the American Revolutionary War. This ship is actually the fourth to carry the name. During the construction of the ship the name was changed when the then current USS Yorktown went down during the Battle of Midway in June 1942. The aircraft carrier that now sets at Patriot's Point earned 11 battle stars and the Presidential Unit Citation during its first tour of duty from April 1943 until January 1947.

After the war ended and after several upgrades were made, the aircraft carrier was recommissioned. It was now an attack carrier when it was commissioned for a second time in January 1953. This time she did her duty in the Vietnam War where she distinguished herself and earned 5 more battle stars. She was decommissioned and retired from battle in June 1970. In 1975 the attack carrier was settled in Charleston at Patriot's Point and opened as an amazing museum and is a National Historic Landmark.

This formidable ship amazingly enough survived through two wars, but suffered no major damage during battles. During her service she also took part in the recovery of the Apollo 8 Space capsules. And as if that weren't enough, another unusual quality of the Yorktown is the frequent reports of paranormal activity.

73

The Yortown from the deck

About the Ghosts

Many people ask me, if there weren't any major attacks on the ship or many lives lost during war, why would it be haunted? Well, when you think about the number of people who have served on this ship and spent so much time on board, it makes sense that there might still be some residual energy aboard this ship. The men took pride in their job and in their ship.

There have been many reports of strange sounds in the belly of the ship. Mysterious clinks and banging are heard as if someone was working on a part of the engine. Skeptics say that this is just normal sounds of an old aircraft carrier settling in the water. However, when the disembodied clinks and bangs respond to questions or oblige when asked to repeat, it's hard to rule it out as natural causes.

My Yorktown Experiences

My first time on the USS Yorktown was an eventful one. As I have stated before I like to get away from tour groups and get a feel for different locations from time to time. When I went below deck and was walking down the hall I saw a man pass in front of me, about twenty feet ahead. He went from the right to the left and went through a doorway. He appeared to be a naval officer in khaki dress pants with a short sleeve buttoned up shirt and stripes on his shoulders.

I thought to myself, how cool is that, and headed in the direction where I saw the man go. I was thinking he was a reenactor whom I could speak with. I wanted to ask about a few things regarding the ship. When I got to the room I saw him enter, he wasn't there. There were no other doors or windows for him to have exited through. I entered the room and all I felt was a major cold spot in the center of the room. The temperature change stood out even more considering the time of year (being summer in Charleston). So why was there such an extreme cold spot here? I found no air conditioning vents or other man made means to describe the phenomenon, but as an investigator I knew this was a common occurrence in some "active" sites.

After returning home from this Charleston trip I did a little more research. I discovered to my surprise that many have encountered the apparition of the same man I saw, matching my description to a "T". It was a great experience for my first time on this beautiful ship. I have been back more than once since, but haven't had a trip as exciting as the first one.

In June 2014 we joined the USS Yorktown Ghost Tours and our guide Patrick Schwab was amazing. He was so full of knowledge and respect for this ship it was fantastic. His ghost stories were a major bonus and when I shared my experience with him, he said that several of their staff and guests had seen the male apparition as well. Patrick also described the fact that recent ceremonies and festivals on board the ship had stirred up the spirits. Especially the events involving surviving WWII seamen.

The USS Yorktown still offers ghost tours at night. These tours provide a great way to see the ship and maybe even have a paranormal experience for yourself. However, if you are among the faint of heart, stick with the historic stuff during the day and just hope you don't run into the ghostly officer many have encountered.

The Yortown at night and an unusual light anomaly, one of these is the moon.

FAIRFIELD COUNTY'S WITCH
Fairfield County Courthouse, Winnsboro, South Carolina

Life in early America was difficult. In some cases those who were different or flourished through difficult times were sometimes branded witches. A woman named Mary found this out for herself near the area that became the Fairfield County Courthouse in Winnsboro, South Carolina.

The Historic Courthouse

Fairfield County Courthouse was built in 1823 by Robert Mills. He was the same man who designed the Washington Monument in Washington DC. It was a point of pride for the residents, but the area had an earlier, more unsavory history. The details of which would forever cast a dismal shadow over the glory of the courthouse building and its construction.

The Courthouse Area and the Story of Mary

Sometime during the 1800's (as the story goes), a woman by the name of Mary Ingelman lived in the area. The townspeople for some reason thought that Mary was a witch and practicing the black arts. She was the first woman in the state of South Carolina to be tried for witchcraft, found guilty, and then sentenced to death for her crimes.

The old Magnolia tree next to the courthouse seemed like a good enough place to hang her and punish her for her crimes. The townspeople strung the rope, hung her, and left her to die, but one of the men in the town felt bad for Mary (thinking she was unjustly accused). He cut the rope in time before she strangled to death. Needless to say the other townspeople were very unhappy that Mary wasn't left to die. There were many attempts on her life throughout Mary's remaining years. She lived a rough and guarded life surviving her near death, but being treated terribly by the townsfolk who hated her so. It's no wonder with the treatment she got in life that Mary would come back after her death and haunt the area of the courthouse and that old magnolia tree.

Mary's Ghost

Mary's energy is most often reported late at night when most people have already gone home. Her ghost is seen on the steps of the courthouse, walking down them towards the magnolia tree. Perhaps she is looking for revenge on the people who tried to kill her and why, or perhaps she is looking for justice and trying to clear her good name. We may never know.

CARNTON'S SPIRITS OF THE SOUTH

Carnton Plantation and Battlefield, Franklin, Tennessee

The Civil War was by far the most painful and disruptive event to the spirit of this young nation since the Revolution. Brother fought brother and homes and homesteads were divided. The lasting scars of that tragic war are still very much a part of the decedents of the soldiers and the buildings that stood quiet witness. If walls could talk then Carnton Plantation and Battlefield would have much to say.

Carnton's History

Carnton Plantation was built in 1826 by former Nashville mayor Randal McGovock. When Randal died in 1843, his son John inherited the farm. He married Carrie Elizabeth Winder in 1848 and they had five children, three of them died at early ages here on the farm.

On November 30, 1864 one of the bloodiest battles of the Civil War was fought here, the Battle of Franklin. The Confederate Army of Tennessee assaulted the Federal Army entrenched in Franklin. The battle lasted nearly five hours, and 9,500 soldiers were either killed, wounded, captured, or disappeared. Nearly 7,000 of them were Confederate soldiers.

The farm house at Carnton served as the largest field hospital in the area. The

once private home was filled with dead and the wounded. The casualties mounted during the battle and during that evening, until the yard too was filled.

On December 1st, 1864 the bodies of four Confederate Generals killed in the battle were dead on the back porch. Their blood stains and those of the other soldiers can still be seen today in the wood floors of the restored home. Early in 1866 John and Carrie Carnton designated two acres of land next to their family cemetery as a cemetery for the almost 1,500 Confederate soldiers who were killed there in the Battle of

The Back Porch
of Carnton

Franklin. They also helped spearhead the effort to have the men reinterred at the cemetery and their identities and information recorded for posterity. They maintained the cemetery until their respective deaths. It is the largest privately owned military cemetery in the nation.

Widow of the South

Carrie McGavock and the family tended to hundreds of Confederate wounded and dying after the Battle of Franklin. She opened her home to the soldiers and gave assitance as much as possible. Confederate soldiers' blood soaked through carpets and seeped in floors (especially in the children's rooms where surgery was performed) leaving many stains still visible today. Carrie cooked breakfast the next mroning and continued to care for the soldiers.

Even after the soldiers were reinterred Carrie kept safe a record book of their names and identities. It still remains at Carnton. Visitors can see the book on display upstairs at the former residence.

Carrie watched over the fallen and the cemetery for 41 years! Carrie's turn at being a good samaritan and preserving the Confederate soldiers records and graves would immortalize her to many as the "Widow of the South". When she died in 1905 the property stayed in the McGavock family for a time.

The MacGavock family kept the property and owned it until 1911, when the last heir's widow, Susie, sold the property. It was put on the National Register of Historic Places in 1973. In 1977 the house and ten acres were donated to the Carnton Association. They have been vital in raising funds to restore the building and open it to the public.

Carnton's Ghosts

This place isn't filled with just Civil War history, but with Civil War haunts too. Many tourists, locals, and workers have all heard the rhythmic sound of drums as if the battle is about to take place, followed by musket fire. Disembodied voices have also been heard, but no one has been able to make out what is being said.

Misty forms and Civil War soldiers appear before people's eyes. Many even say the four Generals whose bodies were placed on the back porch are often seen there as if they are in the middle of a discussion. Perhaps they are still planning the battle.

Carnton Plantation is a fascinating piece of tragic Civil War history. It is a must see for any Civil War buff. It is also a pretty interesting Historic Haunt.

GENTLEMAN JACK KILLED BY A SAFE

Jack Daniel's Distillery, Lynchburg Tennessee

Elvis, Elvis, Elvis! To some people this is Tennessee's most important claim to fame and Graceland the state's only historic site. However, the Volunteer State is also well known for Nashville, the Grande Ole Opry, Great Smoky Mountains, and more than a tale or two from its population. I've previously written about one of the more famous, the Bell Witch (see Historic Haunts of the South). This time out I'd like to discuss another tale that is arguably just as much a part of Tennessee's personality and history, that tale is of Jack Daniels and his world famous distillery.

Jack Daniels

In Case You Don't Know Jack

Jasper "Jack" Newton Daniel was born sometime near the mid 1800s. His exact age and birth date are unknown as there were no surviving birth records from this area of Tennessee during that time. What is known is that he learned the Whiskey business from Dan Call's distillery. He perfected his craft and developed a unique sour mash Tennessee Whiskey. He opened his own distillery in Lynchburg brewing in an area he called the "hollow". Daniels claimed the free cave water and other local qualities gave his whiskey its special flavor. Daniel's "Old No. 7" brand of whiskey would become his trademark and be known worldwide. Ever the ladies man, local rumor claims it was called No. 7 after the number of girlfriends Daniels had (or alternately the number of the train that carried his barrels). The exact date Daniels began producing his signature blend (like his age), is a little uncertain, but believed to be sometime between 1866 and 1875.

Jack never had any children and never married so when his health started failing he gave his distillery to his favorite nephews Lem Motlow and Dick Daniel in 1907. In 1910, Tennessee adopted a state wide prohibition which made sale or production of alcohol illegal. Lem decided to start distilling in St. Louis, Missouri and Birmingham, Alabama. Jack survived to see this and made it a few more years working and educating Lem until a very strange occurrence happened in 1911. Once morning while in his office at the distillery Daniels was trying to open the safe. Daniels on this day, as on many others, had an issue with the combination; he forgot it. He got mad and in a fit of rage kicked the safe! Daniels ended up getting an infection in his toe. It was so bad that it caused a blood clot which eventually led to blood poisoning and his death. The object of his aggravation was henceforth known as the safe that killed Daniel.

The once extremely eligible bachelor was buried in Lynchburg cemetery. His grave made all the more unique by the two chairs next to it. This was of course reportedly provided to comfort the mourning local women. Daniels deeded the distillery to his nephews.

After Jack's death a lot went on in the world of alcohol. Tennessee's prohibition of alcohol was in place and by 1920 other states were beginning to follow Tennessee's lead. Between 1920 and 1933 Prohibition was in effect all over the country and it stopped the production and sale of booze (legally anyway) via the 8th Amendment of the Constitution.

The end of prohibition saw a slow rebirth in alcohol production as many companies had gone under. By 1938 the production of whiskey had begun again in earnest, but it was short lived. With the demands and requirements of crops and necessities to make it, the US Government banned the manufacturing of whiskey due to WWII from 1942-1946. Jack Daniel's Distillery started back up in 1947 after the war, but they had to contend with the fact that it was still illegal (and still is to this day) to sell in Moore County Tennessee. This meant that it was legal to purchase in the city limits, but not in the county where the city was located. By this time Jack Daniels had gained such notoriety and was such a part of this region that most families had worked here and it was now a Tennessee icon.

In 1947 Jack's nephew Lem passed away and handed down the distillery to his sons Reagor, Robert, "Hap" and Conner. The family tradition continues to grow in popularity. At one time Frank Sinatra, a huge fan of the whiskey (having been turned on to it by Jackie Gleason), had a close friendship with the Jack Daniels salesmen that supplied him. Jack Daniels and the "Old No. 7" whiskey have won the "monde de selection" whiskey award seven times. The distillery liked that number and stopped entering after that. Today Jack Daniels is the oldest registered distillery in the U.S. Several owners later, Jack Daniel's Whiskey is still being made and many wonder if the spirit of Jack is still overseeing it all.

The deadly and possibly haunted safe.

Spirits at the Distillery

There have been several reports of a male shadow figure and apparition seen in the oldest parts of the distillery. Many believe it is Jack making sure everything is still being run properly and the whiskey is being fermented to his liking. The safe is another area where paranormal reports have been documented. Some say they have seen an apparition near the safe. Many wonder if even in the afterlife Jack is still cussing out that safe.

The Jack Daniel's Distillery has even been featured on several paranormal television shows because of the activity. The shows depicted not only reports of apparitions and shadows, but seemed to capture evidence of voices being heard and some people having their names called by disembodied voices. The distillery remains extremely active in the paranormal sense as well the physical sense.

You can actually take a tour of part of the distillery and get an idea how whiskey is produced and apparently get a "buzz" by being around all the alcohol filled barrels. You may even have the opportunity to see the "safe that killed Daniels". People flock here every year to see where the legendary whiskey comes from. Souvenir fans will remember it is legal to buy whiskey within the city limits, but not within Moore County. Paranormal fans will learn that whether you experience a ghost while visiting here or not might depend on how much you sample Mr. Daniel's product. Regardless, the Jack Daniels distillery remains a Lynchburg and Tennessee legend and a lively story. It is definitely a spirited Historic Haunt!

TIPPECANOE AND GHOSTIES TOO

Berkeley Plantation, Charles City, Virginia

The Berkeley Plantation

How far would you go for a nicotine fix? In the early 1600's, England was so desperate for tobacco that King James I granted an over 8,000 acre tract of land in Virginia to four men to grow crops and begin commercial ventures. These men, William Throckmorton, Richard Berkeley, George Thorpe, and John Smythe, were purely in it for the profit, and they were part of the 38 men who left in 1619 to establish a plantation in Virginia. When the men came ashore at the site dubbed Berkeley, they observed the first official "Thanksgiving" in America. Of course this was more of a religious ceremony than the feast-filled day we've come to know still it was an important footnote in American History. While tobacco was one of the main interests in the newly established region, the colonists were probably also thankful for the first distilled Bourbon Whiskey in America produced here as well. The Berkeley residents may have drank a toast to what they dreamed would be a productive, profitable, and successful colony. Unfortunately, the once friendly Indians surprised the colonists in 1622 by attacking them! The survivors retreated to the protection of the Jamestown colony.

The Famous and Tragic Harrisons

Many years passed and once it was reworked the property at Berkeley came to be known as Berkeley Plantation. It also became part of the first eight shires of Virginia. The property would become the traditional home of the Harrison family after its purchase by Benjamin Harrison III in 1691. His son Benjamin Harrison IV (with his wife Anne) built a three story manor house there in 1726 from bricks fired on the Berkeley Plantation. Their initials appear in the date stone over the side door and the building is considered the oldest three story structure in Virginia. Benjamin Harrison V was born here that same year and later would be one of the signers of the Declaration of Independence, and three time governor of Virginia. All of his accomplishments made even more poignant by the Harrison family tragedies that started during his childhood and nearly took his life. During a dark and stormy night in 1744 William Harrison IV and two of his children were trying to shut an upstairs window when a stray bolt of lightning struck all three of them, killing them instantly. Benjamin Harrison V was being held by one of his sisters, but miraculously survived thanks to a doctor who was on site.

Benjamin V's son William Henry Harrison was born at Berkeley in 1773. He would become a famous Indian fighter earning the nickname "Tippecanoe". Later he would be elected the 9th president of the United States in 1841 and was president for the shortest term in history. During his inauguration the weather was cold and damp and he gave the longest inauguration address ever, nearly two hours. He fell sick with a dreadful cold and pneumonia that ended up killing him, less than a month in office. He was the last president born before the Declaration of Independence. His grandson, Benjamin Harrison would become our 23rd President and would die much later from influenza.

Berkeley, the Civil War Stand Out

The plantation remained in the Harrison family until 1842. Twenty years later, Berkeley would gain notoriety during the Civil War in 1862. During that year President Lincoln visited the plantation to review General George McClellan's Army of 140,000 Union Soldiers. "Taps" would also be composed that same year on site while the men were encamped. Berkeley's Manor House would see use as a Union hospital and as such was the site for many tragic deaths of wounded servicemen. Many of whom were reportedly buried on the property. With the tragedies of the Civil War and the Harrison family, it's no wonder Berkeley Plantation has a few ghost stories to tell.

Berkeley's Ghosts

Some of the Harrison family still seems to call the Manor house home, as the spirit of William Harrison IV has been seen and experienced by many. Staff and visitors alike have described seeing his spirit in the parlor (he reportedly moves the chandelier), as well as walking through the main level of the house. Witnesses say they could hear his footsteps going from room to room.

A young girl's apparition (believed to be one of William's daughters) is seen in the room where the tragic lightning strike occurred. According to some reports, the windows of that room will sometimes open and close on their own.

There have also been paranormal accounts of a tall thin man in a Civil War uniform. He is often seen walking along the James River and the plantation grounds. Some say the spirit was a patient who died here when the Manor was used as a hospital. In addition, other similarly dressed apparitions have been frequently reported in various places on the grounds.

Checking it out for myself

In fact, there have been so many reports of paranormal activity like this at Berkeley that I felt compelled to visit myself. I toured the plantation, but never saw any of these apparitions or encountered any other activity matching the reports. However, the house does hold a presence all its own. You can feel that you are definitely not alone. If you're in the area I encourage you to take a step back in time at this Historic Haunt, but if your last name is Harrison or a storm is approaching, be careful.

GIVE ME LIBERTY OR GIVE ME ...THE AFTERLIFE.

Red Hill, Charlotte County Virginia

Red Hill

It's no secret that I am a fan of history (the title of this book might have been a clue). A personal favorite of mine is the great Patrick Henry. Henry was a powerful figure that helped shape our country during its formative years. His words stirred our forefathers to bold action and resound even today in our American way of life.

Portrait of Patrick Henry

History of a Great Speaker

Patrick Henry the great "fiery legislator and orator of the American Revolution" was born in 1736. Most people know him for his "Liberty or death" speech, but he did so much more than that. Henry was also a planter, a lawyer, and was governor of Virginia twice (1st governor June 5, 1776- June 1, 1779 and 6th governor December 1, 1784- December 1, 1786).

Henry was married twice. His first marriage was to Sarah Shelton from 1754 until her death in 1775. They had 6 children together before she died due to mental illness which is now known to have run in her family. His second wife, Dorthea Dandridge, was 22 when she married 41 year old Henry in 1777. They had 11 children together and were mar-

85

ried until his death in 1799.

Patrick Henry bought Red Hill Plantation when he retired in 1794 and occupied it until his death in 1799 (he is buried on the property). When Henry lived here the property consisted of a 520 acre tobacco plantation, the main house, out buildings, and his law office. Today it's in the hands of the Patrick Henry Memorial Foundation and is only 117 acres. In the 1950s and 1960s the foundation restored the law office, preserved Henry's grave, and reconstructed the main house. Striving for authenticity the foundation made sure that

Patrick Henry's grave

several pieces in the law office were original to Henry himself. The foundation also built a museum with many artifacts that tell the story of Henry's life.

My good friend and Historic Haunts Investigations team member, Mark Couvillon, is an expert on Mr. Henry. He has published four books on this great man and used to work and live at Red Hill. In addition, Mark like many other witnesses, has experienced several things that led him to believe as I do, that Red Hill is haunted.

Mark's Paranormal Experiences

While working here many years ago, Mark had a friend come to visit. He gave him a private tour of the property after hours. As they stood inside Henry's law office, Mark and his friend saw a reflection in the window of a man behind them in the room watching them. They knew they were the only people on property. They both turned quickly around to an empty room, but as they did so Henry's closed cabinet door suddenly popped open several inches. and the door swung out. Mark examined the cabinet and could find no explanation and couldn't reproduce the experience.

On another occasion Mark had a different group of friends visit him from New Orleans and they brought their four year old son. Mark again played tour guide and showed them the property .The child quietly followed along until they started to approach the law office. The young boy suddenly began freaking out and screamed that he did not want to go in there because of the man in black with the triangle hat. As I was researching this location for the book, Mark sent (the now adult) boy an email about the experience. All he remembered is he did not want to go in there because of the man in black.

Based on the child's description at the time Mark began to wonder could the child have seen Patrick Henry? He did wear black often and most gentlemen of the time did wear tri corn (triangular shaped) hats. I guess Mr. Henry could appear slightly intimidating to children who were not familiar with the man.

While Mark worked and lived here he often heard footsteps and the sounds of furniture being moved. In every case and in fact with all unusual phenomenon he encountered he sought out a rational cause. As an extended member of my Historic Haunts Investigations team, he used many of the techniques and methods that we use to try and debunk or provide a rational explanation, but in Red Hills case he was unable to do so. Regardless of what he experienced he described his experiences as peaceful and never threatening.

My Own Experiences

During my trip here in 2010, I too felt very much at peace while touring the property. Mark's stories left me completely fascinated especially while standing in front of Mr. Henry's desk in his law office. It did feel like there was a presence in that building, nothing malicious, but something that touched me in its own way. I felt a subtle pressure on my shoulder and a calming presence as if someone were standing behind or beside me putting their hand on my shoulder. It was almost as if Henry

Me Standing Near Patrick Henry's Desk

himself was attempting to connect to me or reassure me. A dear friend of mine and historical interpreter, Michael Pfeifer, has often told me "touch history". I'm fairly certain that while I was at Red Hill getting in touch with history, history touched me.

TUCKAHOE'S UNHAPPY BRIDE
Tuckahoe Plantation, Richmond Virginia

Image of Tuckahoe Donated by Plantation

One of the most prominent families in colonial Virginia were the Randolph's. They were a big part of shaping the habits, customs, and politics of the colony of Virginia and the nation. One of their family estates was built in Richmond at Tuckahoe and apparently at least one family member is not too happy to be haunting it.

Tuckahoe's Early Beginnings

William and Mary Randolph's son Thomas, from Turkey Island, first settled the land in 1714 and was known as "Thomas of Tuckahoe". Thomas would have three children William, Judith and Mary. While Thomas began construction on the property his son William would be responsible for much of the rest and the completion of the property. The north portion was built first in 1733 and the central hall and southern portion in 1740. It was a beautiful plantation with a long tree lines drive way and many out buildings, it was known as "Plantation Street".

William and his wife Maria had four children of their own who unfortunately, were all orphaned by 1745 when both parents died within a year of each other. William had left a will to insure that if anything happened to them their children would be cared for and the plantation would go on. William named his dear friend Peter Jefferson and his wife Jane Randolph Jefferson (who was William's cousin) guardian of the children. Peter and Jane moved to Tuckahoe to care for the plantation and children, but they didn't move alone. They moved there with their son, Thomas…Thomas Jefferson. Thomas spent his youth here and attended the one room school that still stands on the property.

The house stayed in the family for many years and even today continues to be privately owned. Self-guided tours of the grounds are available. In addition, the house itself is available for private tours and may be rented for special events. The ghosts, however, are free of charge.

The Ghost of Tuckahoe

The ghost, who is said to haunt Tuckahoe's halls, is Mary Randolph (daughter of "Thomas of Tuckahoe"). She was reportedly forbidden to marry her true love so the two ran away together. Unfortunately, the family tracked her down and brought her back home. She was forced to marry someone much older whom she didn't love. Some say the entire ordeal drove her insane.

There have been many paranormal reports of Mary's apparition seen walking the grounds of the plantation sobbing, looking sad and depressed. These reports have persisted for years. In most accounts her spirit is encountered in her state of dismay, but once her grief is interrupted by witnesses she vanishes. Others have reported hearing the disembodied sounds of a woman crying. When someone attempts to investigate the sobbing, they find no one. This spirit is often referred to as the "Unhappy Bride".

Whether you experience the ghost of Tuckahoe or not on a visit, you are sure to experience one of my families' favorite Historic Haunts and a fascinating piece of colonial history. The boyhood home of Thomas Jefferson is sizable. Big enough in fact to house a wandering unhappy bride.

THE SPIRITS OF BACON

Bacon's Castle, Surry Virginia

Bacon's Castle

Virginia is full of spooks! Well, in some places anyway. Paranormal phenomenon is encountered at several sites throughout the state. Most of the phenomenon reported matches the stories of many other haunted locations. Bacon's Castle, however, has some rather unusual reports that make this historic structure even more unique.

A History of Bacon

Bacon's Castle is only one of three Jacobean style architectural structures in the Western Hemisphere and is the oldest brick dwelling in Virginia and the U.S. dating to 1665. It also boasts the Oldest English formal garden in North America. The original owners were a very prosperous planter and his wife by the name of Arthur and Alice Allen. After Arthur Allen's death in 1669, he left his home to his son Major Arthur Allen II, who was a Member of the House of Burgesses and a supporter of the Colonial Governor.

In 1676 Nathaniel Bacon and several followers caused an uprising that would become known to history as Bacon's Rebellion. The armed rebellion forces were made up of settlers of Virginia. They were dissatisfied with the political structure, trade practices, and safety of colonists under the rule of the colony's Governor William Berkeley. It would be the first rebellion by discontented frontiersmen in the American colonies. Bacon's forces attacked Native Americans, chased Berkeley from

Jamestown and later burned the capitol. Bacon's men drove Major Arthur Allen from his home and occupied the building (hence the name despite the fact that Bacon himself never reportedly went to the house). The rebellion was eventually suppressed by armed merchant ships and Government forces from England, but it took several years.

It took Allen four more years to get his home back and even longer to get it back to its original state. The property remained in the Allen family until 1844. After that year the house saw a variety of different owners as it was repeatedly sold and changed hands until the 1970s. That's when Preservation Virginia took it over and restored the home, outbuildings, and the 17th century gardens. Bacon's Castle opened up to the public in 1983. The property underwent even more renovations in 2012. Today the renovations are complete and the sight is a popular tourist attraction. However, the renovations seem to have stirred up some supernatural activity which only adds to the location's already interesting story.

Unusual Activity at Bacon's Castle

There have been stories of unusual experiences and encounters reported here for over 300 years! In fact, the passing of comets and other astrological events has typically heralded extreme misfortune. During these celestial occurrences Bacon's Castle and the property have experienced Indian invasions, locust swarms that wiped out crops and damaged grounds, as well as intensified reports of paranormal activity. Among these reports are differing details of disembodied voices and noises, apparitions, and many others.

Like the grounds, the activity in the house seems to differ depending on who encounters it. Still the paranormal encounters reported are numerous. One family of disbelievers came to visit the castle grounds claiming to have heard the "ghost stories". A few moments after their arrival one of the family members fell down the steps of the Castle, swearing afterwards that she didn't trip on anything and that "something" pushed her. Another visiting nonbeliever on a different day claimed to suddenly become deathly ill while on the property. As soon as she left she was fine. These types of unusual experiences are not uncommon and not limited to disbelievers of paranormal phenomenon.

One family of believers stopped by for a visit to the Castle and grounds. When they arrived they were uncertain if the museum was open yet, but when they found the door unlocked went in. They thought it was odd no one was around, but felt very warm and welcomed and started touring the grounds themselves. While standing outside, they watched a gardener walk up to the door and unlock it with her key. They went up to talk with her and told her how beautiful the place was and how they had already walked through and taken a tour for themselves. The woman was shocked and said the door was locked when she walked up to it. There was no way the family visiting could have locked this particular door behind them without the key because you have to have the key to do so. According to several reports this too is common and Bacon's Castle and the grounds themselves seem to have a mind of their own. Many believe if the house wants you in, it will allow you in and if it wants you to experience something supernatural you will.

Bacon's Castle and the grounds have been the subject for years of reports of mystery sounds, footsteps, and include details of an apparition of a lady with white hands. In addition, there are frequent reports of unusual atmospheric phenomenon that many have referred to as dancing or moving balls of light. In fact, at the nearby Old Lawne's Creek Church cemetery (just a few hundred yards from Bacon's Castle) there have been a ridiculous number of matching reports over the years of paranormal activity by variety of guests, employees and others. These reports all detail and describe a red ball of light or fire which rises some 30 feet in the air from the cemetery with unusual movement and activity before it suddenly disappears. Headlights, reflections and other plausible scientific explanations have been explored and discarded.

My Experiences with Bacon

During one of my many trips out to Bacon's Castle while I lived in Williamsburg, I arrived on a day when the building was closed (and this time the doors did not seem to open themselves). Disappointed, I decided to walk around the main house. While standing in front of the Castle something caught my eye up by the chimney. It appeared to be a dancing or floating ball of light. This was during the day and unfortunately I didn't have my camera. I watched it for several seconds before it just sort of shot off out of sight. The sun was in a different position in the sky and I ruled out reflections or other causes for the phenomenon.

Personally, I have always felt the house has a very warm feeling to it, others (especially non-believers who experience being pushed or those who encounter the red lights) may not agree. I have a few friends who are reenactors and they bravely explore history, but hate going inside this place. They claim its due to the uneasy and unnatural feelings they experience while inside the building. Regardless of which camp you fall into, skeptic or believer, (I would hope many reading this book fall into the latter), Bacon's Castle and the grounds remain a historical gem and a site definitely begging for further investigation and exploration.

GHOSTS ATTENDING THE COLLEGE
The College of William and Mary, Wren Building, Williamsburg Virginia

The Wren Building

Its no secret that I am a great admirer of Williamsburg, Virginia. The area is rich with history from Colonial Williamsburg to the College of William and Mary. As a fan of history, geneology, and the paranormal, the area holds a special place in my heart. My ancestors lived in Williamsburg and in some cases attended class in William and Mary's hallowed halls. While there are numerous reports of paranormal activity on campus, one of the most frequently haunted buildings on campus seems to be the Wren Building.

History of the Wren

On February 8th, 1693, King William II and Queen Mary II of England (my tenth great grandparents) signed a charter for a "perpetual college of divinity, philosophy, languages, and other arts and sciences". It would be founded in the colony of Virginia. The town of Middle Plantation where the college would be located would later become known as Williamsburg in 1699.

Construction began on the Christopher Wren Building in August 1695 by contractor Thomas Hadley and with the designs of its architect for whom the building was

93

named. The Wren Building is the oldest academic structure in the United States still in use. The Wren Building burned three times. Each time the building was reconstructed. The original exterior walls were incorporated into the rebuilds. The current structure dates to 1732. The Chapel within the Wren was constructed in 1729 by Henry Cary Jr. and is located on the south end of the west hall. Services were first held in 1732 and there is a crypt located under the chapel room where the graves of Governor Botetourt, Sir John Randolph (my ninth great grand uncle), Peyton Randolph (my first cousin ten times removed), along with several other Virginia notables resides.

The College of William and Mary is the first US institute with a Royal Charter, first Greek Letter Society (Phi Beta Kappa founded in 1776), and the first law school in the country. Classes at William and Mary and its Wren Building were attended by several greats including; Thomas Jefferson (my second cousin nine times removed who's Monticello was featured in my second book Historic Haunts of the South), James Monroe, John Tyler, and John Marshall who are all former presidents. George Washington received his surveyor's license there at the age of 17 and was a chancellor at the college at one time.

William and Mary is also one of the few colleges that had to cancel classes due to the "British Invasion" during the Revolutionary War. During the Battle of Yorktown the Wren was used as a hospital for French soldiers fighting during the war. Following the war the Wren Building, and the college itself, returned to the business of education. In 1906, the college became a State institution. In the 1920's, Dr. W.A.R. Goodwin, with the support of John D. Rockefeller, began the ambitious Williamsburg restoration project. The Wren Building was the first major building restored.

Ghosts of the Wren

While there are tales of ghostly incidents during the restoration, incidents of the paranormal have been reported at the Wren building for literally centuries. Ghost stories and paranormal occurrences have repeatedly been reported and published nationally and locally in a variety of campus publications. Many students and staff report hearing footsteps, especially on the upper levels of the Wren building. Some people believe it is the ghost of Christopher Wren himself. Others believe it is the French soldiers who died here when the building was used as a hospital during the Revolutionary War.

Its hard to determine the true origins of the Wren building's spirits, but a possible contributing factor to the paranormal activity could have been the students themselves. Steam tunnels play an important part in supplying the college with heat, internet access, cable television and other conveniences. For decades there have been persistent rumors by faculty, staff, and students of steam tunnels connecting through the "basement" of the Wren building and its crypts. There are reportedly at least 9 secret societies on campus, and most not only know of these tunnels, but supposedly encouraged fraternity brothers to sneak into the crypt and steal bones. There could be a connection between these disturbances and the activity in the building.

Exploring the Wren for Myself

One of my first experiences at William and Mary occurred when I was about 8 years old and entered the main building. It felt like I had been there before and I felt completely at home there. When I returned many years later as an adult, I experienced the same comforting feeling.

During my tour as an adult, the entire time I visited the college (especially the Wren building) I felt like someone was with me. Maybe one of my ancestors who once attended the college centuries ago was touring the campus with me. I often heard footsteps directly behind me, but when I turned to see who was there, I found no one. This happened every time I was inside the Wren (and I went back to visit several times).

So Just Who Haunts the Wren?

Some people believe the spirits buried within the Wren chapel are the ones haunting this building. Others still maintain the ghosts of Christopher Wren or the Revolutionary War heroes haunt the building. Evidence gathered frequently by many paranormal investigation groups have made it no less difficult to narrow it down to a specific ghost or to several. We may never know exactly who haunts these historic halls, but if you want to hear about more of the ghost stories at the most beautiful college in America (in this humble writer's opinion) you will have to wait till Historic Haunts of the South III is released. One more note about the College of William and Mary from me, "GO TRIBE!"

THE GHOSTS OF PEYTON'S PLACE

Peyton Randolph House,
Colonial Williamsburg Virginia

Peyton Randolph House at Colonial Williamsburg

Genealogy, as I have mentioned before, is a passion of mine. While tracing my own families lineage I was happy to discover we were direct descendants of the Randolphs of colonial Virginia. The Randolphs were one of the first and more prominent members of colonial society and they would have a profound effect on our newly shaping free country. Thomas Jefferson was only one member of the Randolphs who would effect the early America. So I was only too happy to include details of paranormal activity at the most recognizable Randolph homestead, the Peyton Randolph House.

The History of Peyton's Place

The Peyton Randolph House is named after Peyton Randolph. Randolph was a Virginia statesman who would become the Speaker of the Virginia House of Burgesses and the presiding officer of the First Continental Congress at Philadelphia in 1774. The west wing of the house was originally built in 1715 by William Robertson. Sir John Randolph purchased the west wing in 1721, bought the empty lot to the east in 1724, and constructed another building there. This Randolph (a distant ancestor of mine) was the only colonial born in Virginia to be knighted. John died in 1737 and left the house to his wife Susannah Beverly Randolph until their second son Peyton turned 24 years old. Their other children inherited other properties in and around the tidewater area.

When Peyton moved into the home with his wife Betty, he built a main house in between the two already existing structures. The west side was connected to the main house but the building to the east was not. It is believed that this building was used as an office.

Peyton's mother lived in the home with him and his wife until her death in 1754. The home became a political hub as the Revolutionary War drew near. Peyton unexpectedly died of natural causes in 1775, and because they had no children, left the house to Betty. Betty opened up the former residence to General George Washington and French General Rochambeau when they arrived in Williamsburg where they planned out their strategy in 1781 for the siege at Yorktown.

After Betty's death the house went up for auction in February 1783 and changed hands many times through the years. The east wing of the house was demolished sometime in the 19th century. It wasn't until the Colonial Williamsburg Foundation got a hold of the property in 1938 that the restoration and reconstruction begin. Between 1938-1940, an amazing amount of work and renovations went in to what you see today. Further restorations occurred in 1967 resulting in the opening of the center and west portions of the house in 1968. In 1997 more of the out buildings were reconstructed.

My Experiences with the Randolph House

This is one of my favorite buildings owned by the Colonial Williamsburg Foundation and one of the most haunted. When I lived in the historic area I would often go sit on the lawn across from the Randolph House at night and just watch the activity taking place before my eyes this despite the fact that there would be no one in the building. A ghostly candle would often appear in a window and you could watch it illuminate different rooms on the second floor. The security alarm has frequently been known to go off from time to time on its own while the house was vacant. At times like these security guards would often arrive and find no one in the building, the alarm functioning correctly, and that nothing had been tampered with.

On the second floor one of the bedrooms has frequent reports of unusual paranormal occurrences on a regular basis. In fact, some of this activity I have witnessed myself. In most accounts a perfectly made bed in an otherwise empty room will appear to have been laid in or sat on. This only a few seconds after someone has left the room and come back. Despite the lack of living people present to explain it in most of these accounts there is a definite indention in the bed. Other guests and employees have witnessed this phenomenon numerous times. Other reports of the building by these same employees and guests describe feelings of dread or uneasiness in some of the rooms.

I spoke with a former employee and friend who wants to remain anonymous and he told me he used to get creeped out when he had to close the building at night by himself, especially in the winter months when it gets dark earlier. These tales are relatively tame and just the tip of the iceberg. The Peyton Randolph House has been dubbed by some the "most haunted building on the east coast". Over the years it has reportedly been the site of several children's deaths from illness or accident. It has also seen adult suicides, tuberculosis deaths, and other unfortunate and tragic occurrences. It's no wonder than that apparitions have been reported here for over 200 years! In addition, employees and guests have reported recurring disembodied sounds of shattering mirrors and heavy footsteps. Many visitors have reported encountering the apparition of a white shimmering male figure in the house that disappears. Employees on many occasions have reported encountering a young man in colonial garb mistaken for another employee or reenactor who suddenly vanishes into thin air.

While I have returned to the building on several occasions I have not shared these particular experiences (with the exception of the footsteps). This could be because of my ties to the Randolphs, circumstance, or just random coincidence. One thing is for certain though this historic gem in an amazing piece of the nation's history with many historic and haunted stories to tell.

GLADSOME GHOSTS IN WILLIAMSBURG
George Wythe House, Colonial Williamsburg Virginia

George Wythe House in Colonial Williamsburg

Virginia has always been a birthplace for followers of democracy and liberty. Many of our founding fathers have ties to this amazing state. One of the more fascinating men of this era to me has always been George Wythe.

The History of Wythe and the Wythe House

George Wythe (pronounced with) was a leader of the Patriot movement in Virginia and a delegate of the Continental Congress. He was Virginia's first signer of the Declaration of Independence, and the first "American" law professor. He even taught law to another one of our "founding fathers", Thomas Jefferson, at the College of William and Mary.

Before the events that led to the American Revolution, George married a woman named Ann who tragically died in August of 1748, eight months after they had enjoyed their Christmas season nuptials. After this the widowed George dedicated himself to a life of law and scholarship. He continued successfully practicing law before moving into the legislature. Later, George again married, this time to a woman named Elizabeth. Most historians believe Wythe's father in law, surveyor and builder Richard Taliaferro designed and built the couple a house in the mid 1750's with many extra features unusual in houses of the time.

99

The house is a two story brick structure with four rooms on each floor. In addition the structure boasted a smokehouse, kitchen, laundry, and several others that gave the Wythes amenities that many others didn't have. A touching gift from a father in law.

While living in the house Wythe would gain a reputation for radically opposing the Stamp Act of 1765 and other efforts by the British to regulate the colony. He also served as Williamsburg's mayor (1768-1769) and was elected by fellow parishioners to the vestry of Bruton Parish Church (1769). As the situation with England grew worse Wythe joined the militia and served with distinction in several capacities including as Virginia's delegate to replace George Washington once he took command of the continental forces (Wythe's house would even serve as Washington's headquarters prior to the siege of Yorktown). Wythe would later prove instrumental in helping Virginia establish its seal (still used today), state law system, the important new republic concepts of religious freedom, public records access, court systems, and education. His student, Thomas Jefferson, was influenced greatly by Wythe's efforts and remained his closest friend and confidant.

While pursuing the many noteworthy accomplishments that makes him a famous historical figure, George and his wife Elizabeth lived together in their home for over thirty years. In 1787 Elizabeth died and George moved to Richmond in 1791. In Richmond Wythe would serve as judge in Virginia's Court Chancery. After many other remarkable successes in law and teaching Wythe was reportedly poisoned by a relative and died in Richmond in 1806. He was buried in St. John's Episcopal Church.

The Fate of the Wythe House

Wythe's home would pass to his heirs and change hands several times. In 1926, Reverend W.A.R. Goodwin of Bruton Parish Church, just next door, made his office on the 2nd floor after acquiring the Wythe House and turning it into the parish house. Dr. Goodwin, the "Father of Colonial Williamsburg" began his restoration project on Williamsburg soon after. Colonial Williamsburg obtained the property in 1938 and restored the interior in 1939 to a form reminiscent of the Wythe years.

The Ghosts of the Restored Wythe House

There are several spirits thought to be frequenting the Wythe House. Ironically enough, Rev. Goodwin, while alive, made several references to the Wythe House ghosts before his spirit too became one of its more renowned haunted residents. After Dr. Goodwin took over the Wythe House in 1927, he made a comment, "shut your eyes and see the gladsome ghosts who once made these places their home. You can learn to call them back."

In 1936 during the restoration project a women wrote to Dr. Goodwin about a story she had heard about three ghosts haunting the Wythe House. His reply was, "they are very elusive ghosts and refuse to be delineated or described within the limits of any paragraph. The only way is to come here and hold communion with them."

Another time, Goodwin wrote, "I am in the Wythe House waiting for the hour to strike for the midnight Christmas Eve service…one is not alone here. The ghosts of the past are my gladsome companions in the near midnight silence." Rev. Goodwin may have summed up his opinions on the paranormal in the best fashion when he was quoted as saying, "I wouldn't give a hoot for anybody who doesn't believe in ghosts."

Goodwin's strong belief in the paranormal might explain why his own spirit is one of the most commonly reported in the Wythe House. Many report the presence of Dr. Goodwin in his office, especially late at night. Cold spots are often felt in that room. Many visitors outside the house have described seeing a man looking down from the window late at night when the house is known to be empty. I have also seen interesting things coming from that same room when I lived in Williamsburg. While I lived in Williamsburg I enjoyed late evening walks through the historic area. One night while passing the Wythe House I felt as if someone was watching me from an upstairs window, so I snapped a picture (I usually take my camera with me when I travel). When I reviewed the photo, there was a strange ball of light in front of that same window. Perhaps it was Dr. Goodwin?

Besides Rev. Goodwin's spirit there are a multitude of other reports of paranormal activity at the house. Candles are often seen flickering in the windows, that quickly go out. This happens most often when there are no candles present in the house. In addition, voices are often heard throughout the house even when empty. Others have reported the presence of a female spirit in the house as well. She seems to walk down the hallway and straight through the wall. This phenomenon has been witnessed and reported by several visitors to the home.

A male apparition in colonial garb has also been seen walking up and down the stairs. Based on appearance and description several people claim that this is the ghost of George Wythe. Even though he was poisoned and died in Richmond it seems he may have returned to his former home in Williamsburg.

The Wythe House seems to be serving as a home for many souls just as it did in life. Whether the spirits are George Wythe, his second wife Elizabeth, Reverend Goodwin or something else entirely, the Wythe House is one Colonial Williamsburg's most paranormally active locations. The kinds of activity the Wythe House seems to support would suggest that for some history really can come alive. It's easy to see why this is one of my favorite Historic Haunts.

Unusual Light Anomalies at the Wythe House

ABOUT THE AUTHOR

Jamie Roush

Jamie Pearce lives in Jacksonville, Florida with her husband Deric and their cat Griffon. With over 19 years of experience in the paranormal field and four books under her belt, Jamie Pearce is obviously a fan of the paranormal. However, she has a passion for more than history and the paranormal, she is also a scuba diver and avid runner. As a child she wanted to be a marine biologist and a fitness trainer. Even though her career path went in a different direction, she still has a passion for the ocean and being fit.

Another passion of hers is traveling and she has many new locations in mind for the future that she and her husband will hopefully be visiting. Ideally they will be featured in upcoming books. Pearce currently has three more books in the Historic Haunts series in progress and is always looking for new and exciting haunted locations. She continues to post the evidence of her investigations and research of the paranormal through her website **www.historic-haunts.net** and with her team **Historic Haunts Investigations.**